RETURN OF IMAGINATION:
J.R.R. TOLKIEN'S OTHER WORLDS

by

Shari G. Grant

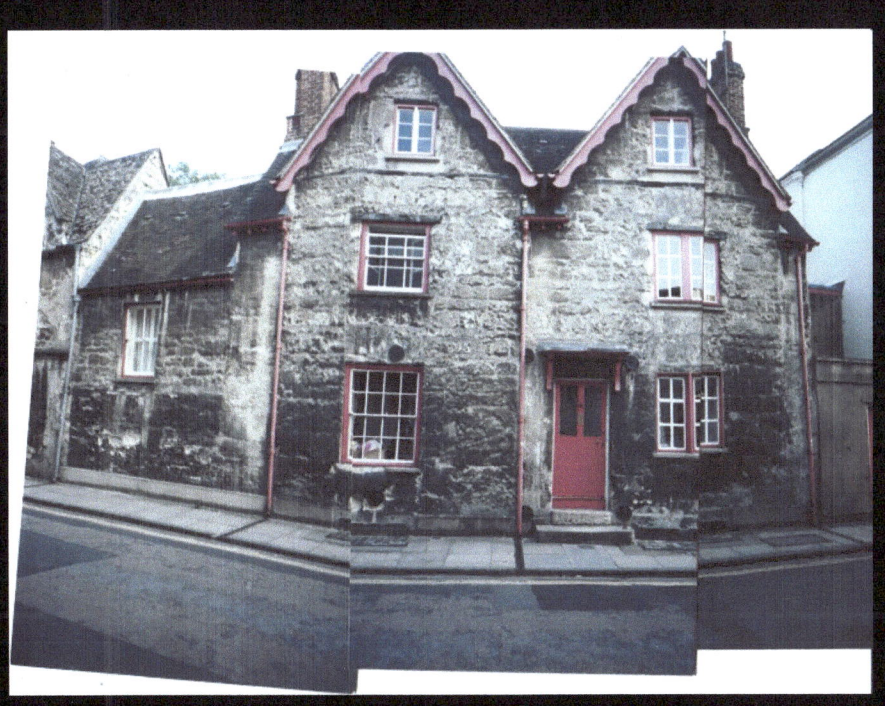

With gratitude
to

Shannon, Jeneane & Spirit
and others of Middle Earth
for the return of my imagination

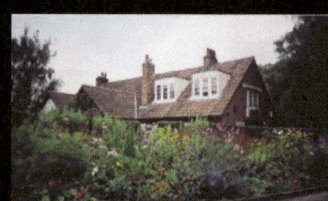

LIBRARY OF CONGRESS
CATALOGUING-IN-PUBUCATION DATA

GRANT, SHARI G.
RETURN OF IMAGINATION: J.R.R. TOLKIEN'S OTHER WORLDS

I. CREATIVE PROCESS 2. TRANSCENDENCE I. TITLE
ISBN 1451571240
ARCHITECTURAL PRESENCE PUBLICATIONS
P.O. BOX 173
DEL MAR, CA 92014

FIRST EDITION PUBLISHED AUGUST 2004
SECOND EDITION PUBLISHED MAY 2009
THIRD EDITION PUBLISHED JULY 2011

RETURN OF IMAGINATION: J.R.R. TOLKIEN'S OTHER WORLDS

**Exploring the creative process
through nature and imagination**

by
Shari G. Grant

ENRICH YOUR LIFE
AND
RETURN TO YOUR IMAGINATION

In his Prologue to Lord of the Rings, Tolkien describes Middle Earth as being located on our Earth, in some quite remote epoch of the past. Tolkien states that "Hobbits ... are still here, and though they hide from us in their silent way, some of us have sometimes seen them and passed them on as names in our folklore." Who has not sensed the presence of a Leprechaun, a Menahune, or a Fairy - or at least wished to catch a glimpse of the little people?

TOLKIEN-LIKE CHARACTERS ARE IMAGINED
IN THIS BOOK IN THE VERY WOODS OF OXFORD
WHERE THEY WERE CREATED

CHARACTERS

GOOD GUYS

- ents
- entwives
- great eagles
- horses
- elfs
- dwarfs
- hobbits
- wizards
- river maidens
- unique individual
- talking beasts

BAD GUYS

- wizards
- nazgul
- orcs
- urk-hai orcs

BOTH GOOD & BAD

- hobbit descendant
- human

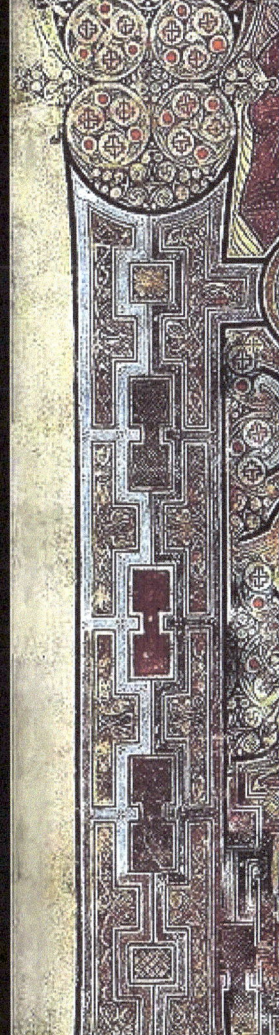

Book of Kells illustration Circa 800

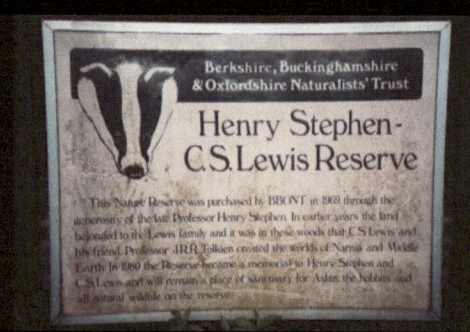

Picture two tweed-vested Englishmen walking through their beloved woods, talking about "Faerie" - C.S. Lewis, undoubtedly puffing on his proverbial pipe and J.R.R. Tolkien perhaps dialoging with Hobbits around him in the woods. Tolkien would have ridden his bicycle over to Lewis' home (both men lived in Headington, a suburb of Oxford) during the writing of the *Lord of the Rings*.

Tolkien's habit was to get together frequently with his close friend Lewis. In addition to scheduled meetings with their literary group, the Inklings, the two authors repeatedly met for lunch at Lewis' home. Located near the firing kilns of old Brickworks, Lewis' home named the "Kilns", is adjacent to a beautiful wooded area called Shotover Hill.

On walks after lunch they read and critiqued their current writing projects, sharing ideas and gaining inspiration from each other. Imagine them on these walks tromping through the woods. Their combined vision inspired the creation of Hobbits and the many creatures and other worlds that are now so familiar to readers of their novels. Turn the pages to begin to imagine and to see what they might have seen....

GOOD GUYS

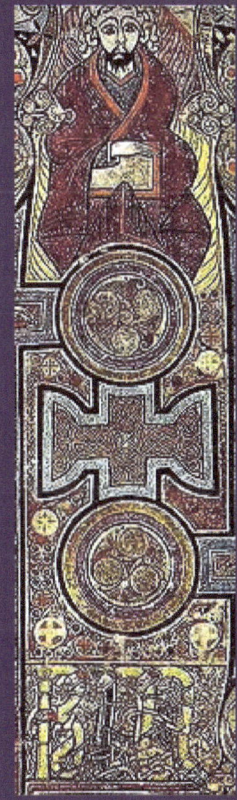

Book of Wells illustration
Circa 800 (public domain)

ENTS

I saw his face the minute I walked past him on the path leading up the hill through the nature reserve on Shotover Hill. Often I would watch others as they strolled by and wait for them to notice the Ent's face. No one else seemed to realize he was there, watching – watching.

He became like an old friend, and as our affections deepened, I noticed more of the details of his physical appearance: the mossy eyebrows, the leafy hair, the eyes with many years of wisdom, the limbs reaching down into the earth, and the strong swaying overreaching presence. He led me into the world of "Faerie" and gently freed my imagination to see other characters in the woods.

Tolkien-like characters eventually became visible to some of my friends in these enchanted woods after being introduced to this magnificent Ent!

---- Intelligent Species, Nature ===

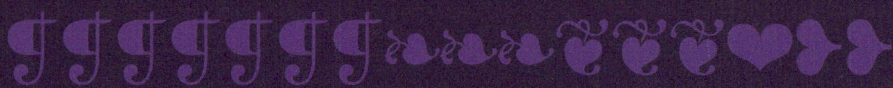

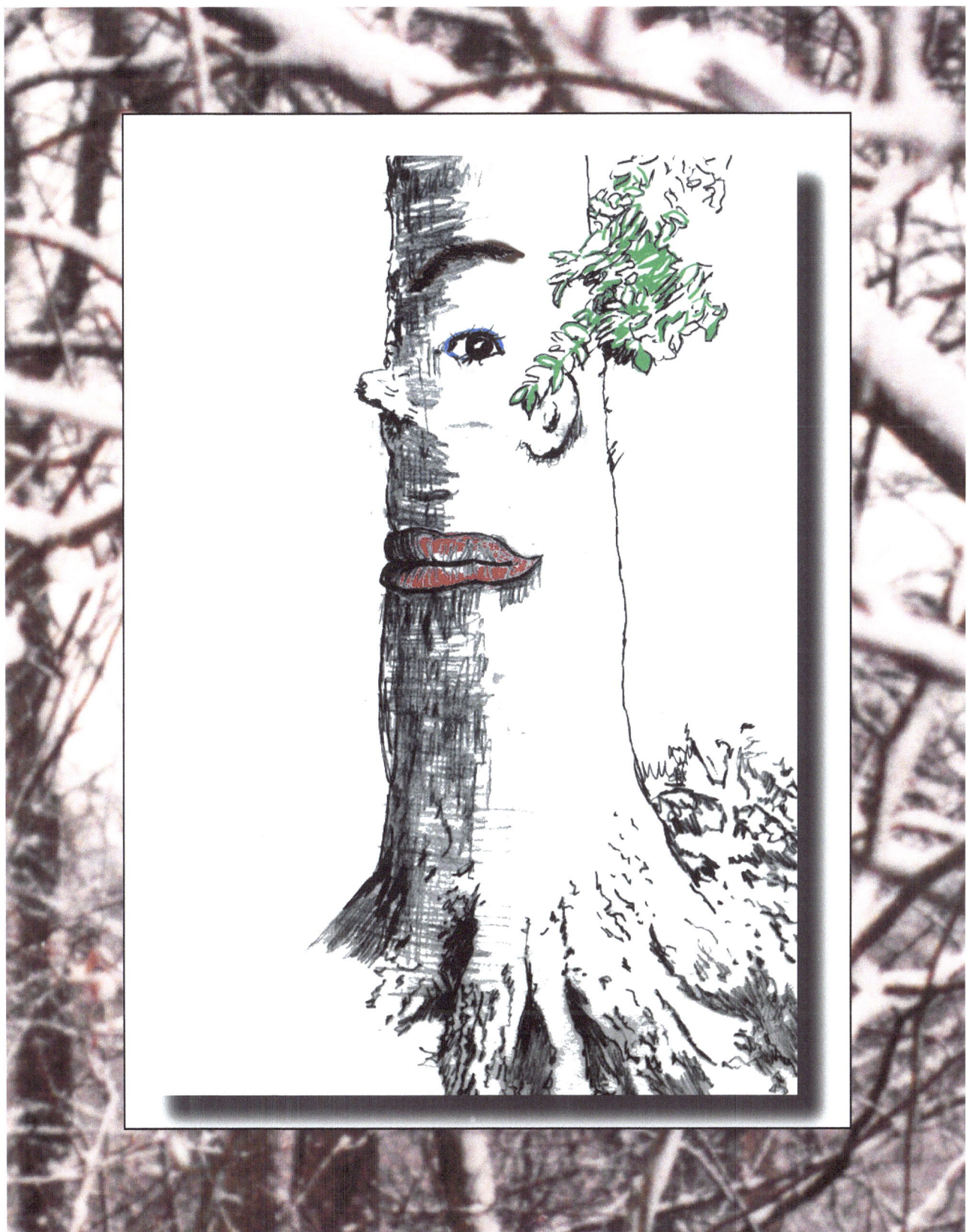

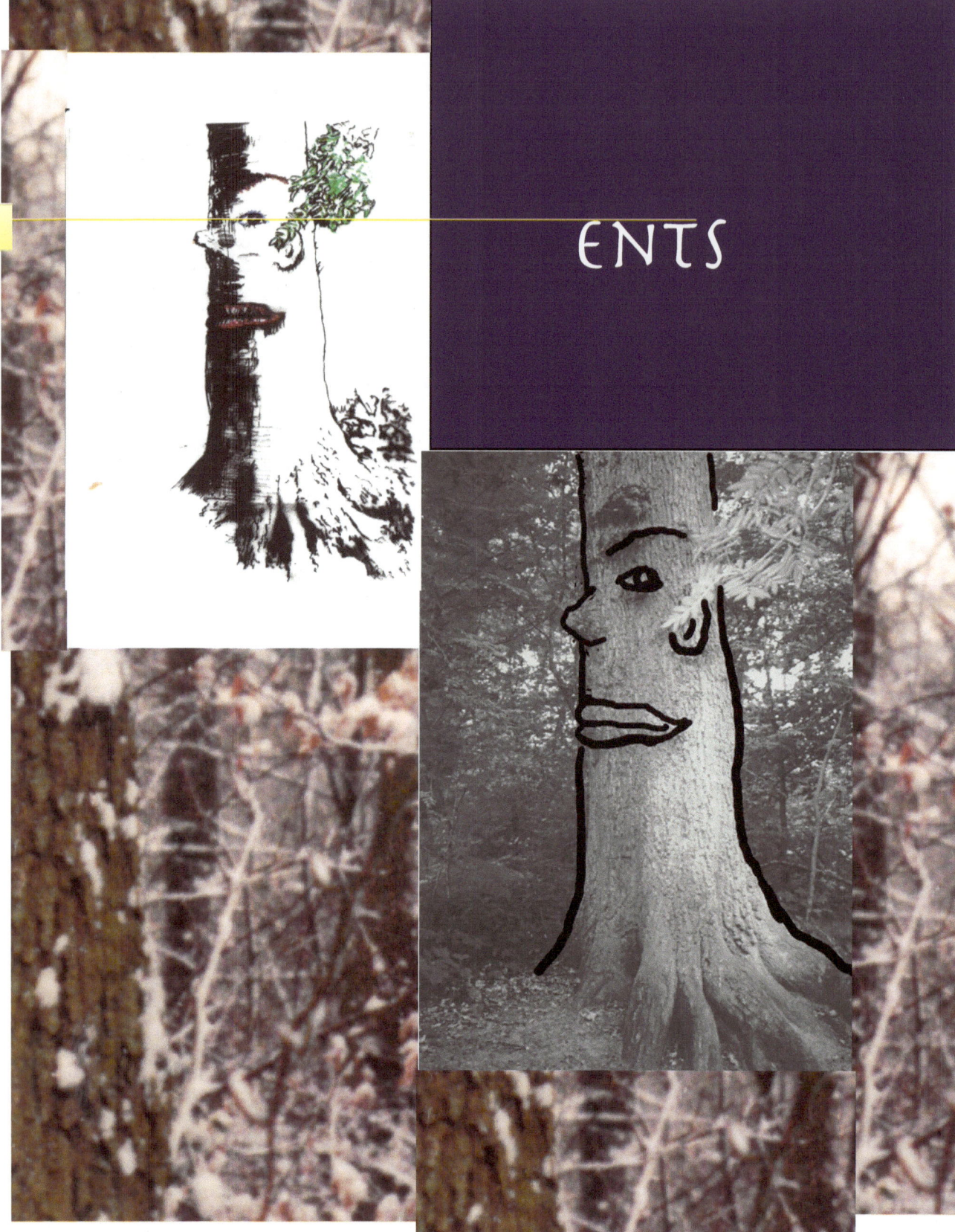

ENTS

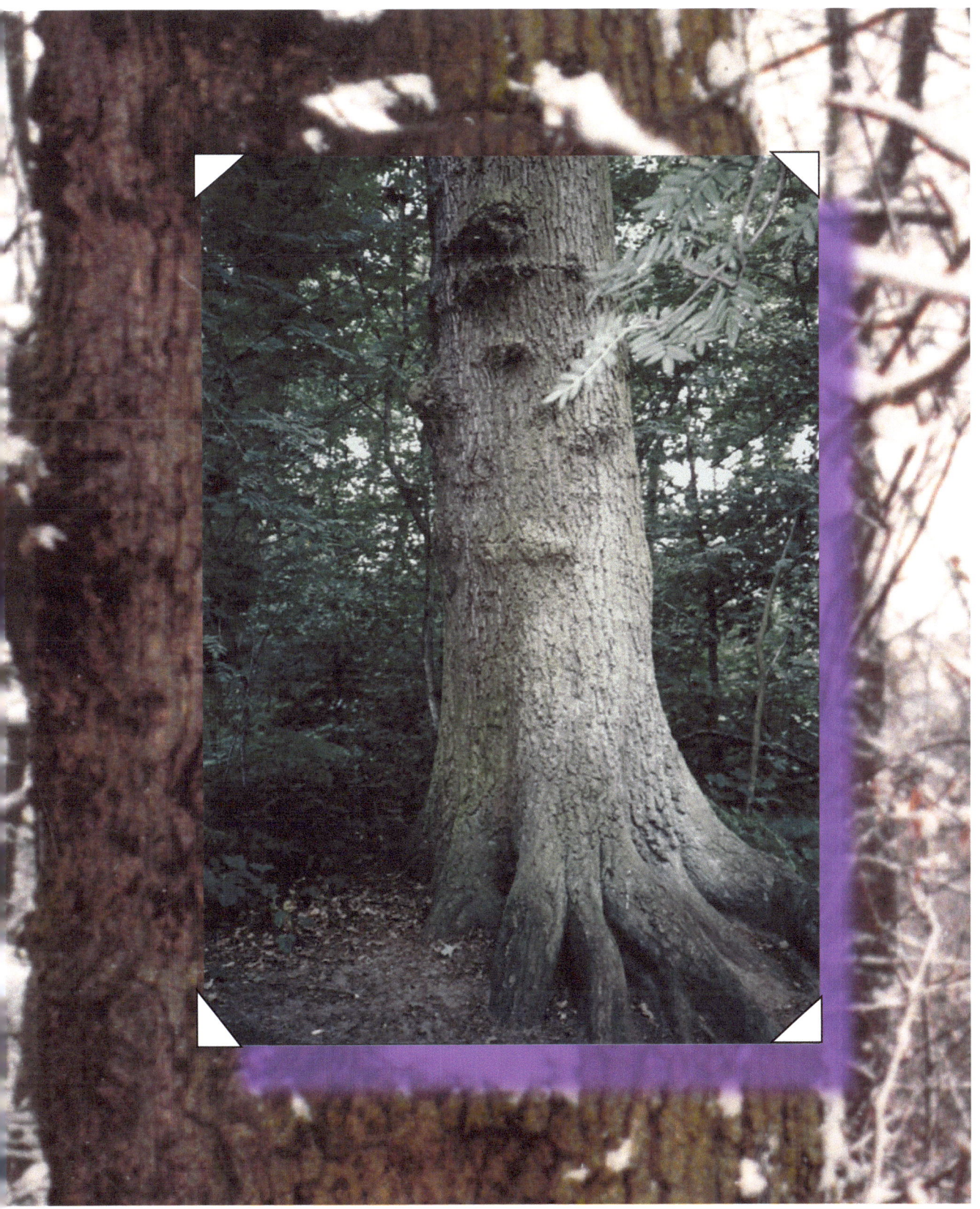

ENTWIVES

As you wind your way through the dense vegetation in the nature reserve on Shotover Hill, the path switches back and forth until it opens into a clearing in the trees.

One day, while standing in the center of the circular area surrounded by trees, we found our imagination drifting to what had gone on in this place many times over years past. The pulsating energy from the dancing and whirling that has permeated this celebratory circle can easily be felt. The Dionysian energy is unmistakable. Closing our eyes, we began to see the Ents moving, and the Entwives swaying with the intoxication of the dance.

Paul and Tanner felt the magic also and began a pas de deux ,doing a lift with Tanner's subtle back arching gracefully in a backward motion across Paul.

There was a collective gasp as we looked up and saw the same move repeated by a watching Entwife.

---Misdirected, Nature ---

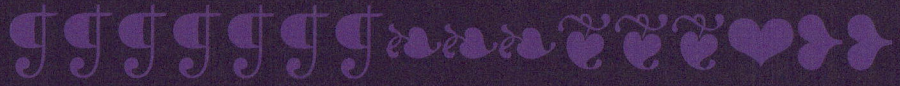

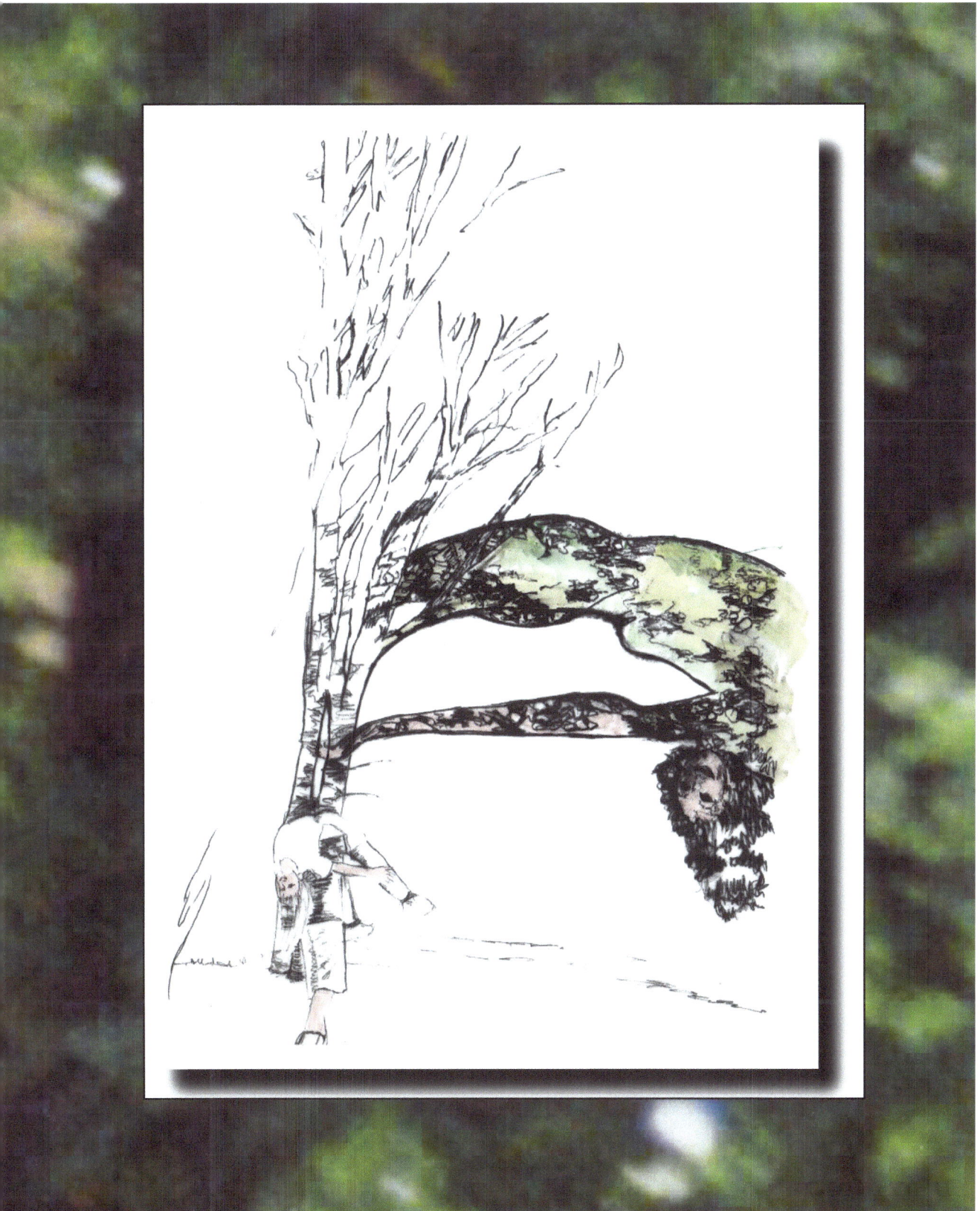

ENTWIVES

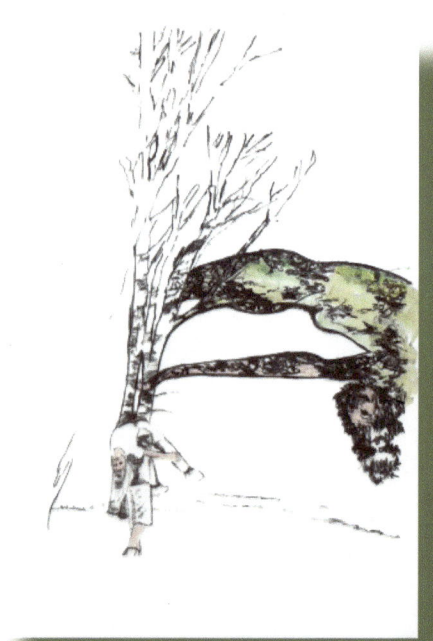

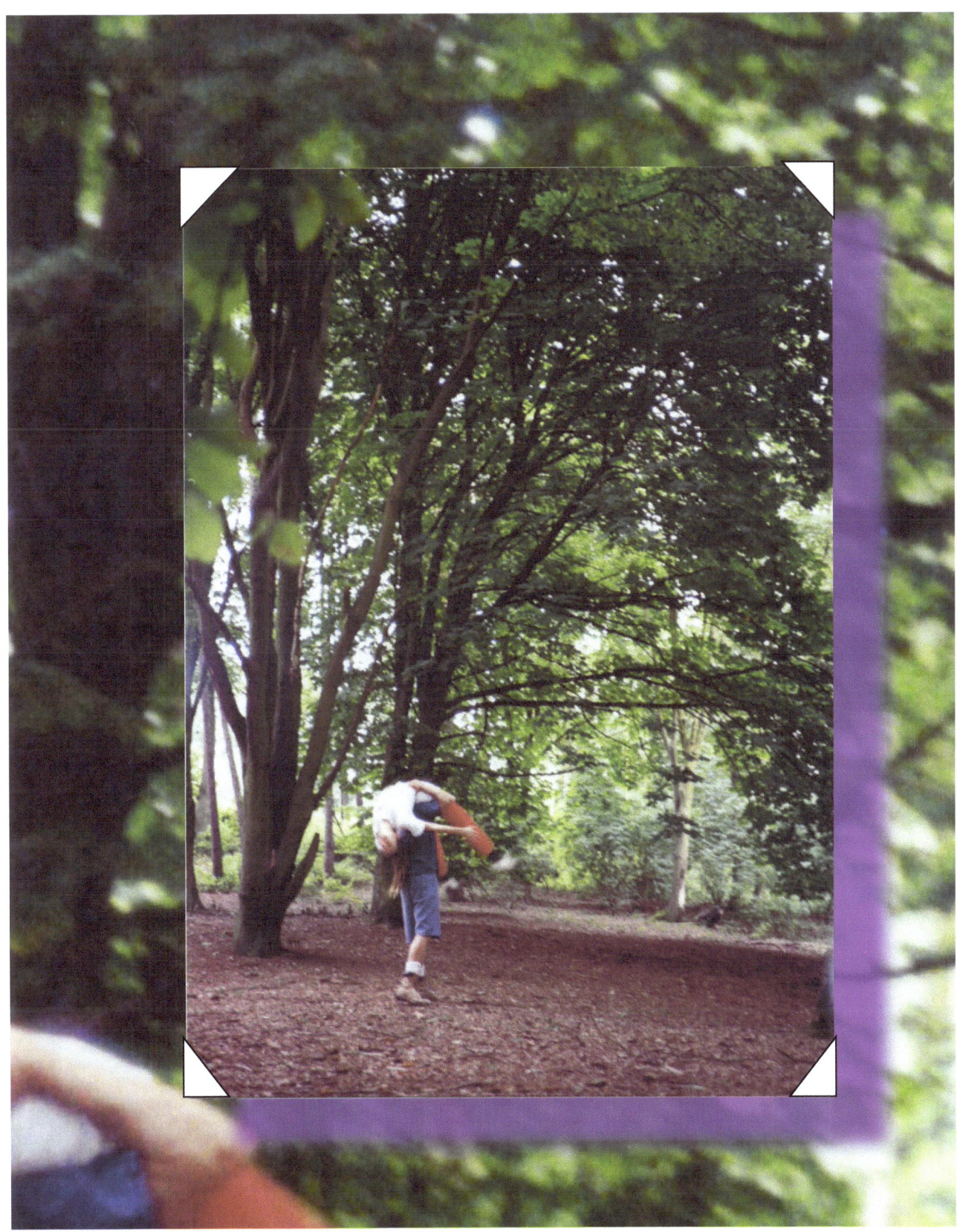

GREAT EAGLES

If your good sense leaves you one day and you find yourself held by the arms of the welcoming forest, lying on your back on a soft green carpet of vegetation, gazing up at the sky filtered through the branches of the trees, you may see things that you never guessed you would.

The sounds of little birds and crickets may be joined by the sound of flapping wings. Just above the top of the enormous ferns you may see winged creatures on an apparent rescue mission. Great Eagles can sometimes be seen, soaring very low and looking almost like shadows, to avoid being detected in the crystal balls of the evil forces.

--- Noble, Rescuing ---

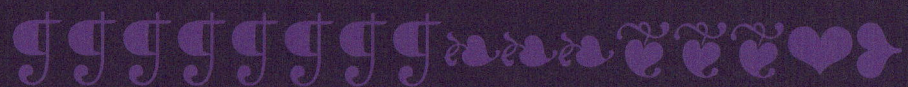

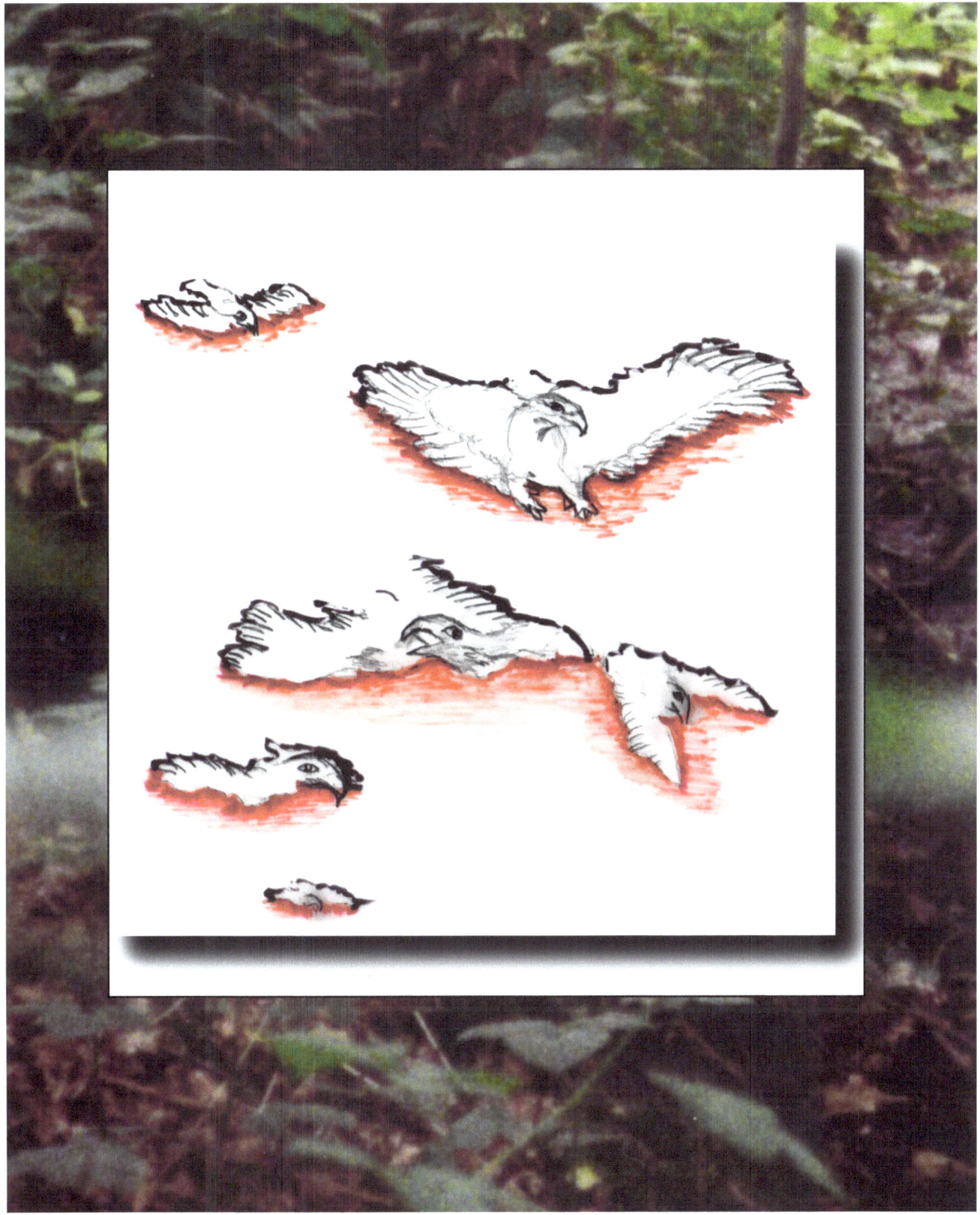

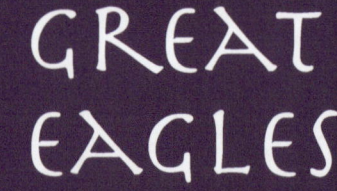

GREAT
EAGLES

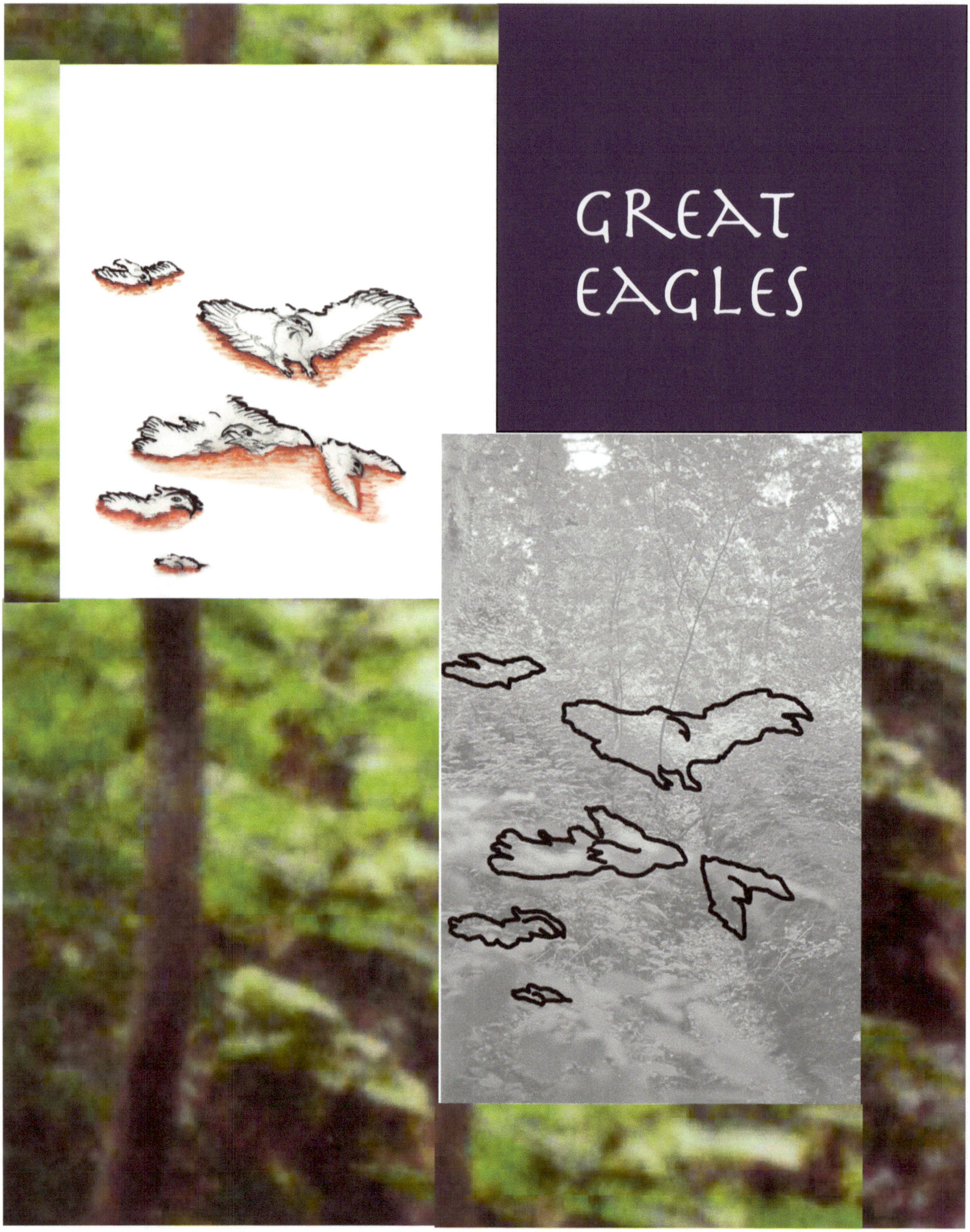

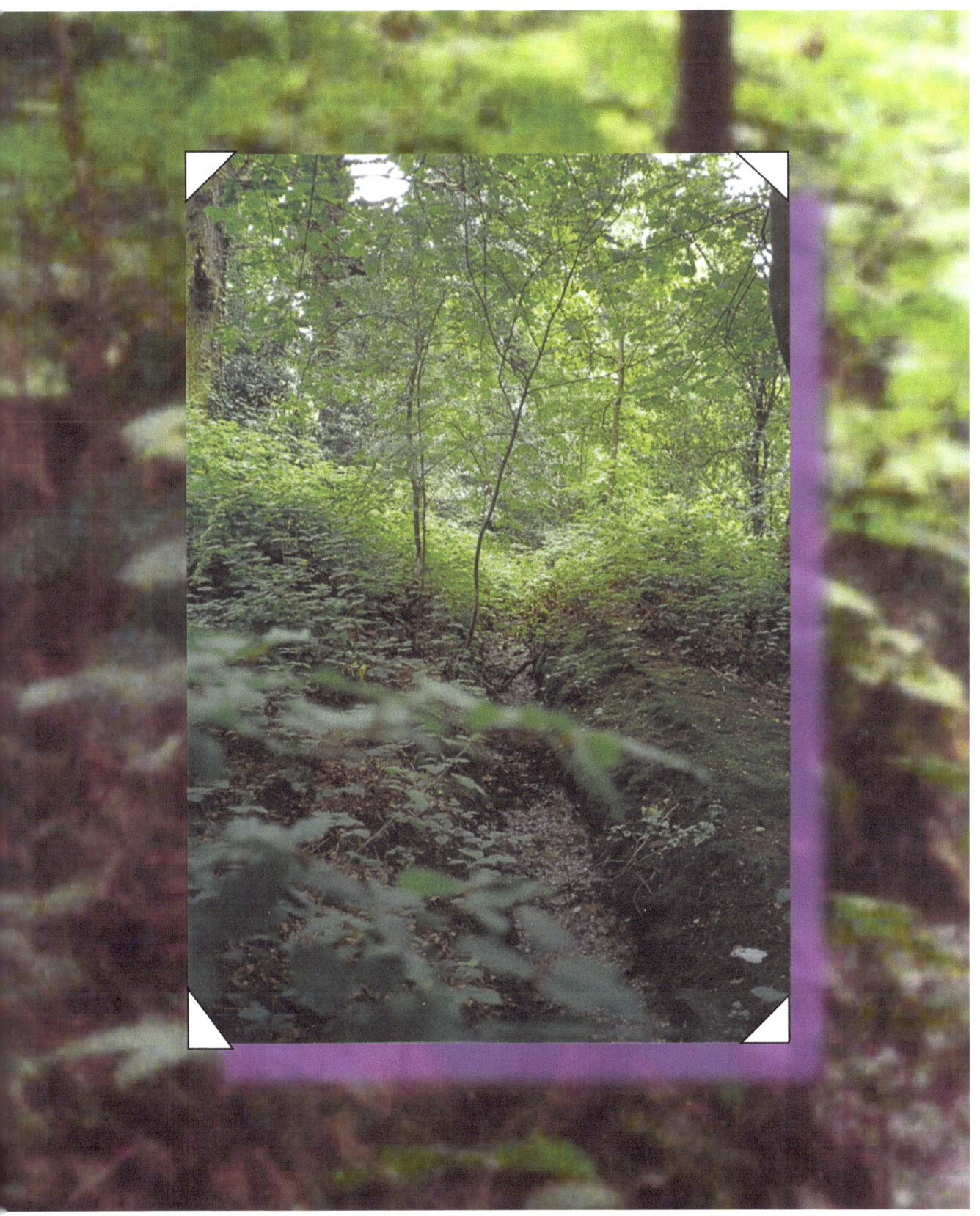

SHADOWFAX

If you walk through the graveyard next to Holy Trinity Church In Headlington, you may see the simple concrete slab marker of C.S. Lewis and his brother Warnie. Lewis' special gift of encouragement and persistence hi the bond of friendship is the reason Tolkien completed the Lord of the Rings trilogy.

From the grave you can look over to the adjacent grassy field and see horses grazing. Possibly, if you study the trees along the edge of the field you might catch a glimpse of Shadowfax - flying at top speed through the sky or taking off unexpectedly through the trees.

-- Specially gifted, Unicorn like ---

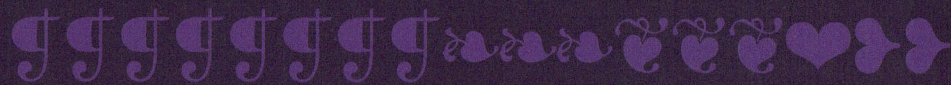

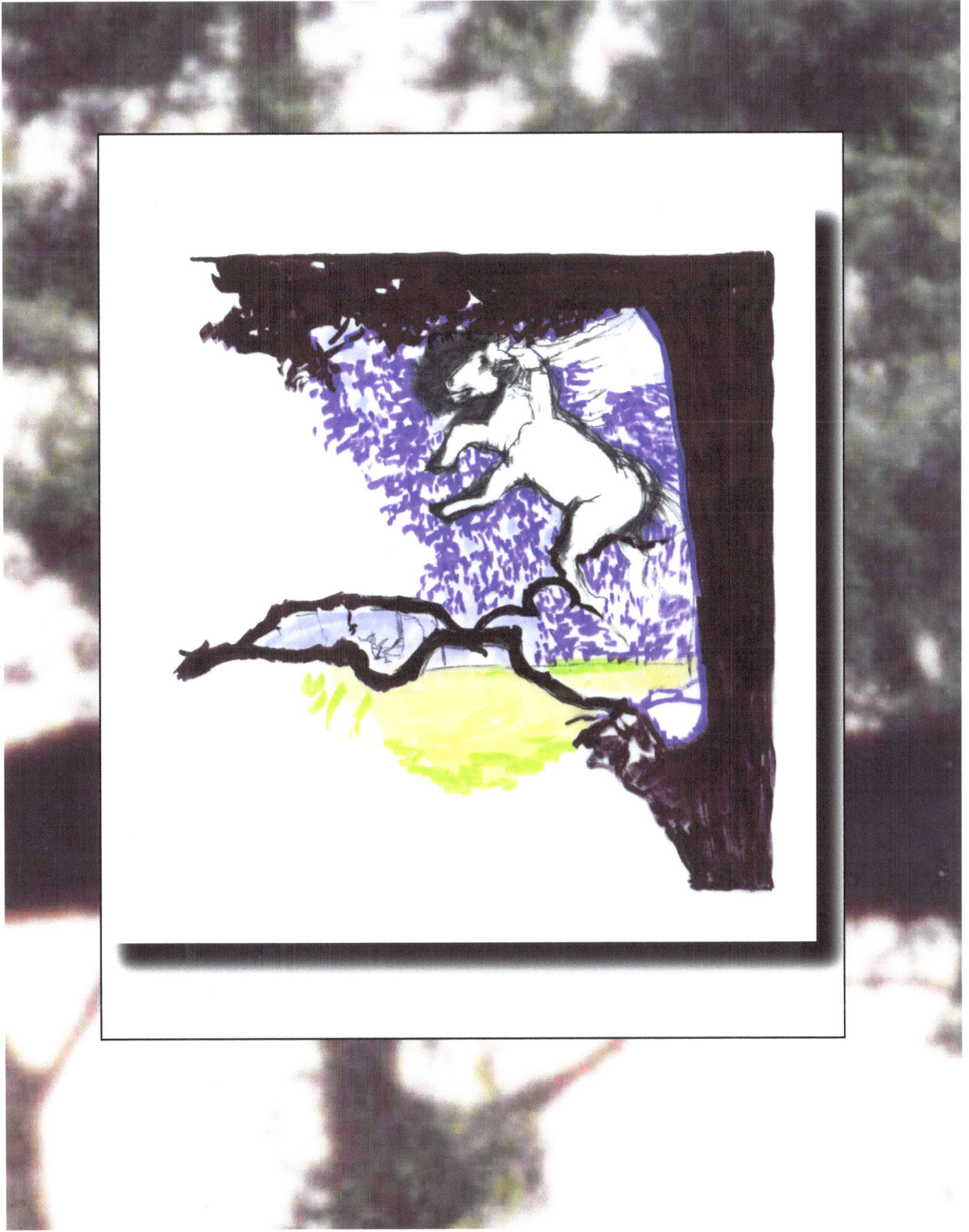

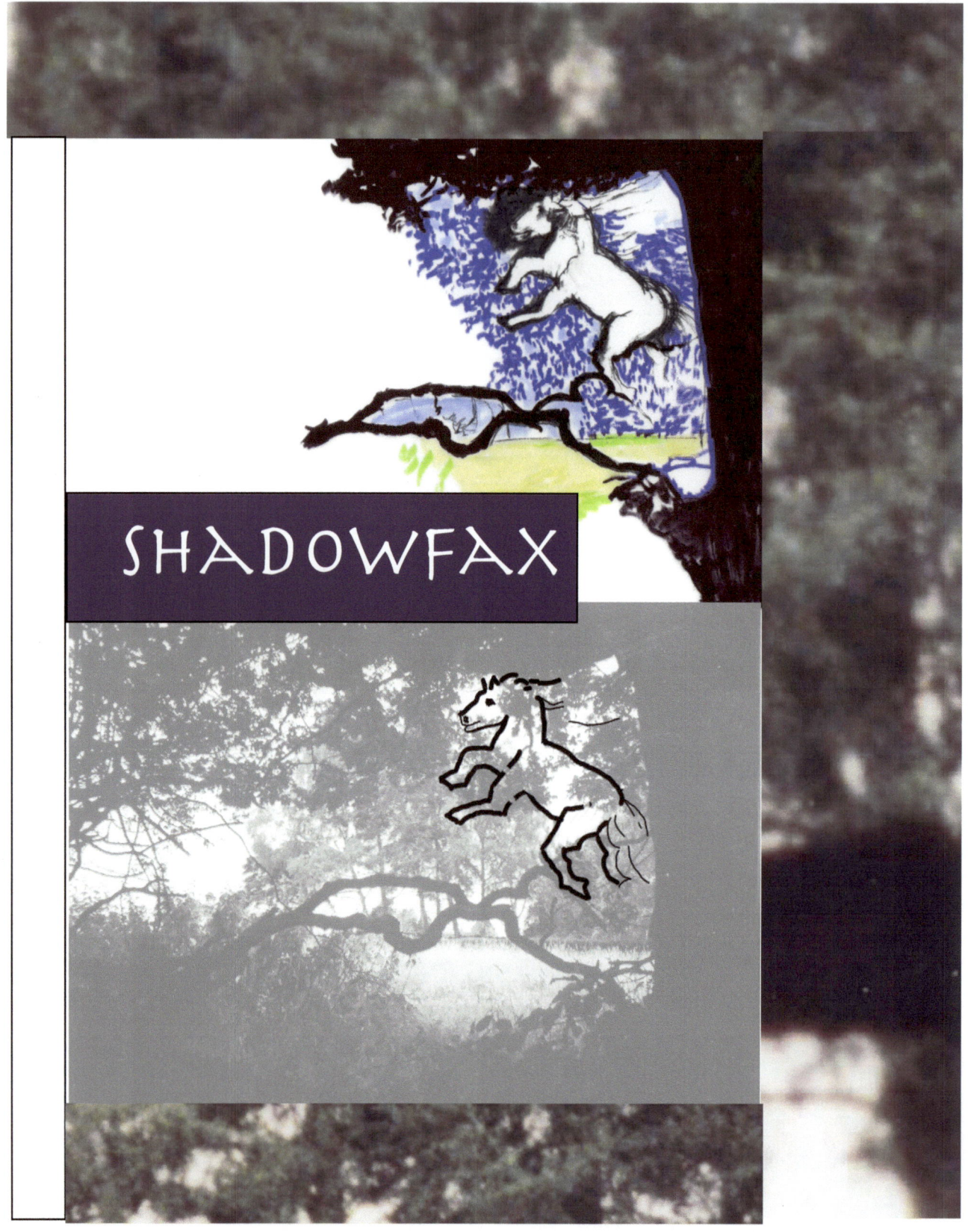

SHADOWFAX

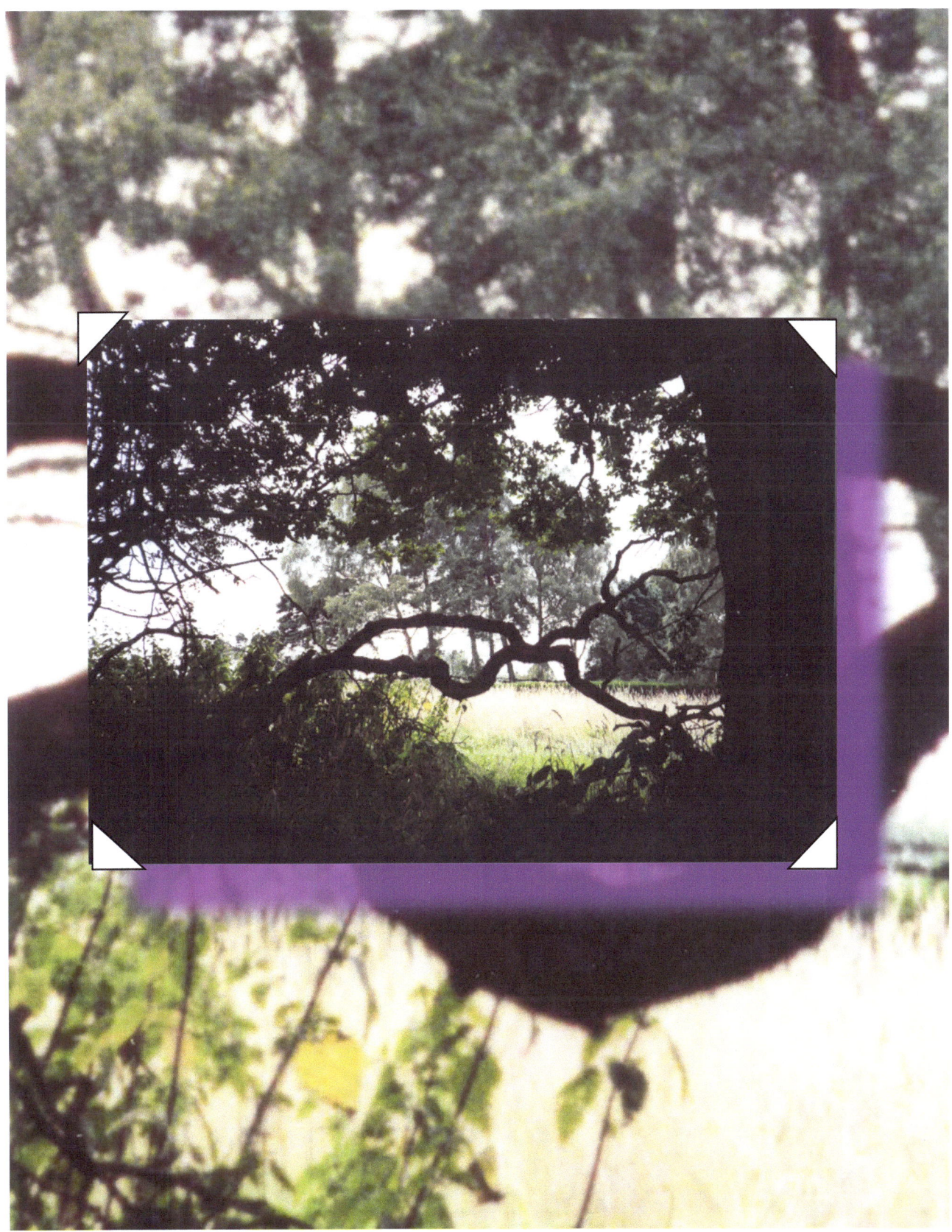

GALADRIEL

As you walk into the nature reserve and look directly ahead, you may see the sun streaming down onto the pond and lighting up a tree standing out in the water.

Sometimes the light radiates so strongly from the tree that it seems as if the light source were coming from within. Focus on the area of the brightness and see if there might be a movement, even ever so slight.

As strange as it seems, the light may be coming from one single source - a ring on the finger of a hand in the midst of the tree. The light shone similarly in Riviera when Galadriel passed the test of resisting the incredible power that would have come to her had she kept "the one ring", in addition to her own.

--- Light, Serenity, Compassion ---

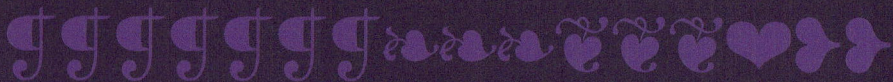

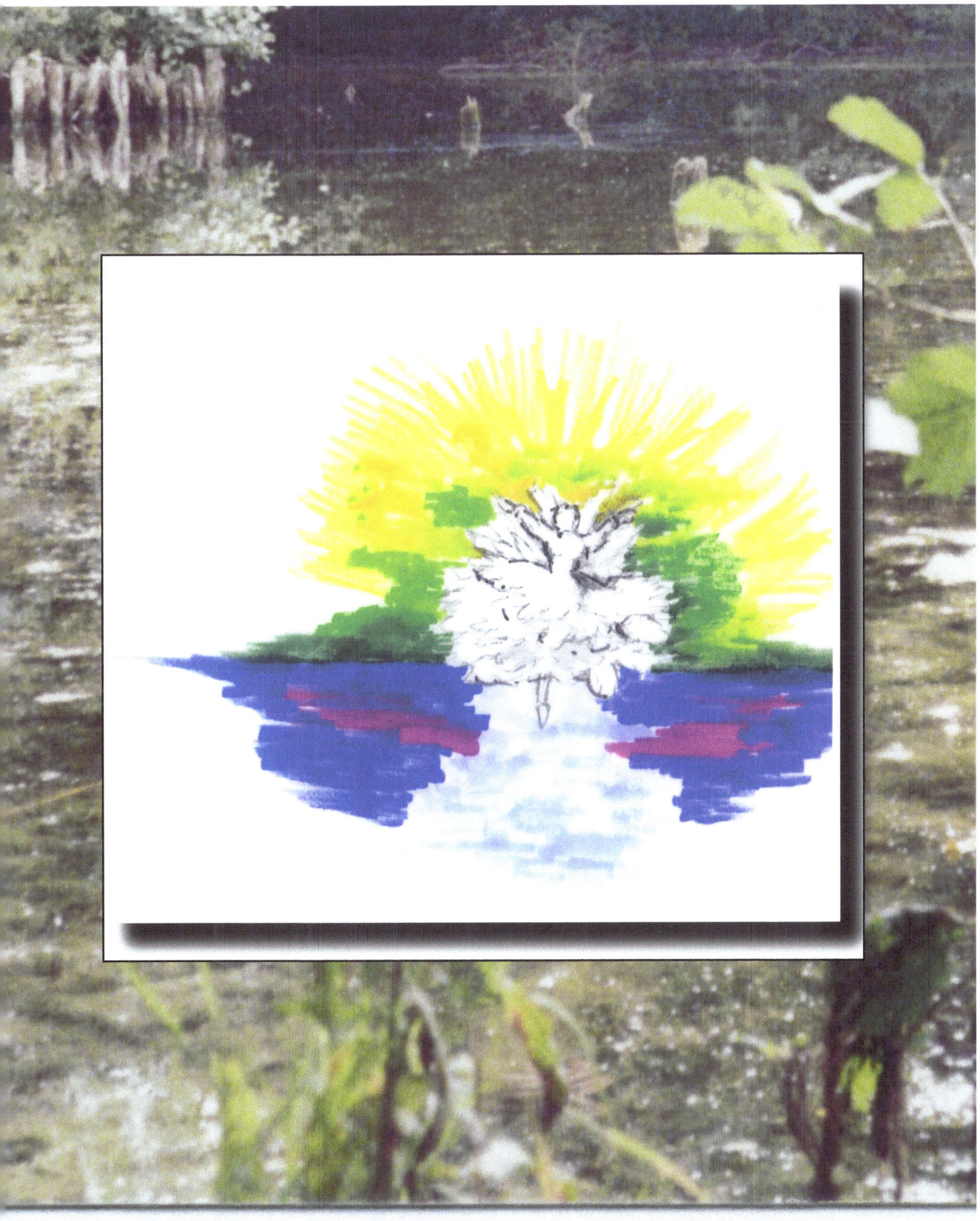

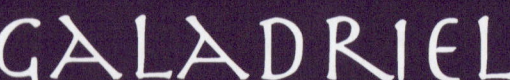

GALADRIEL

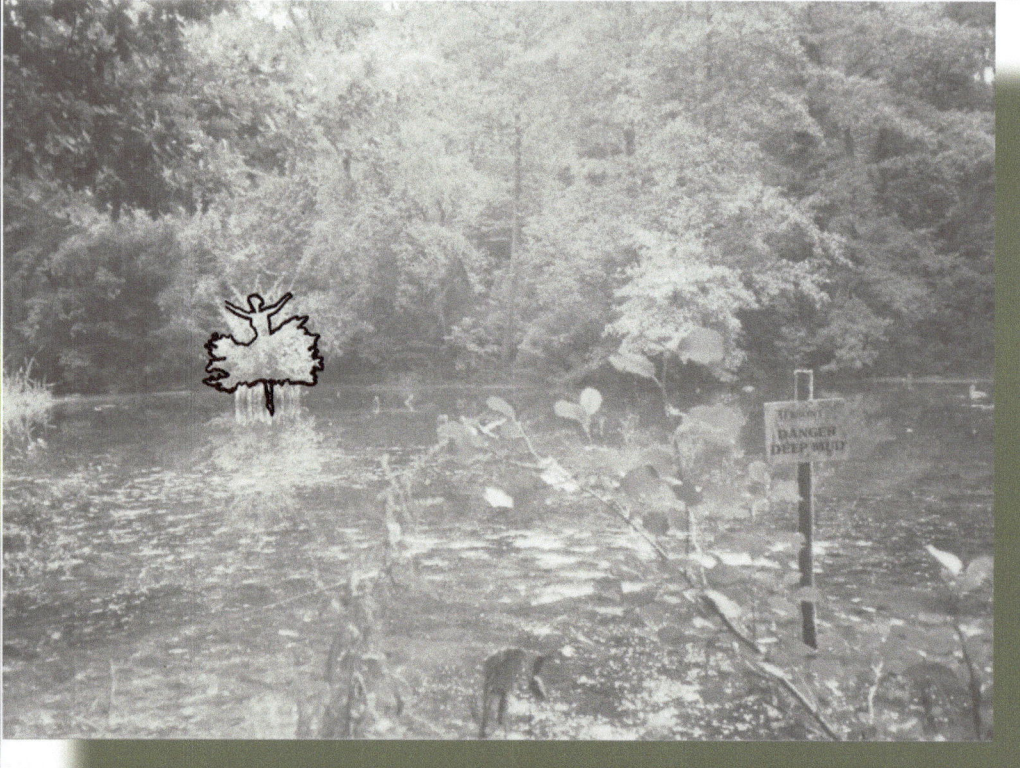

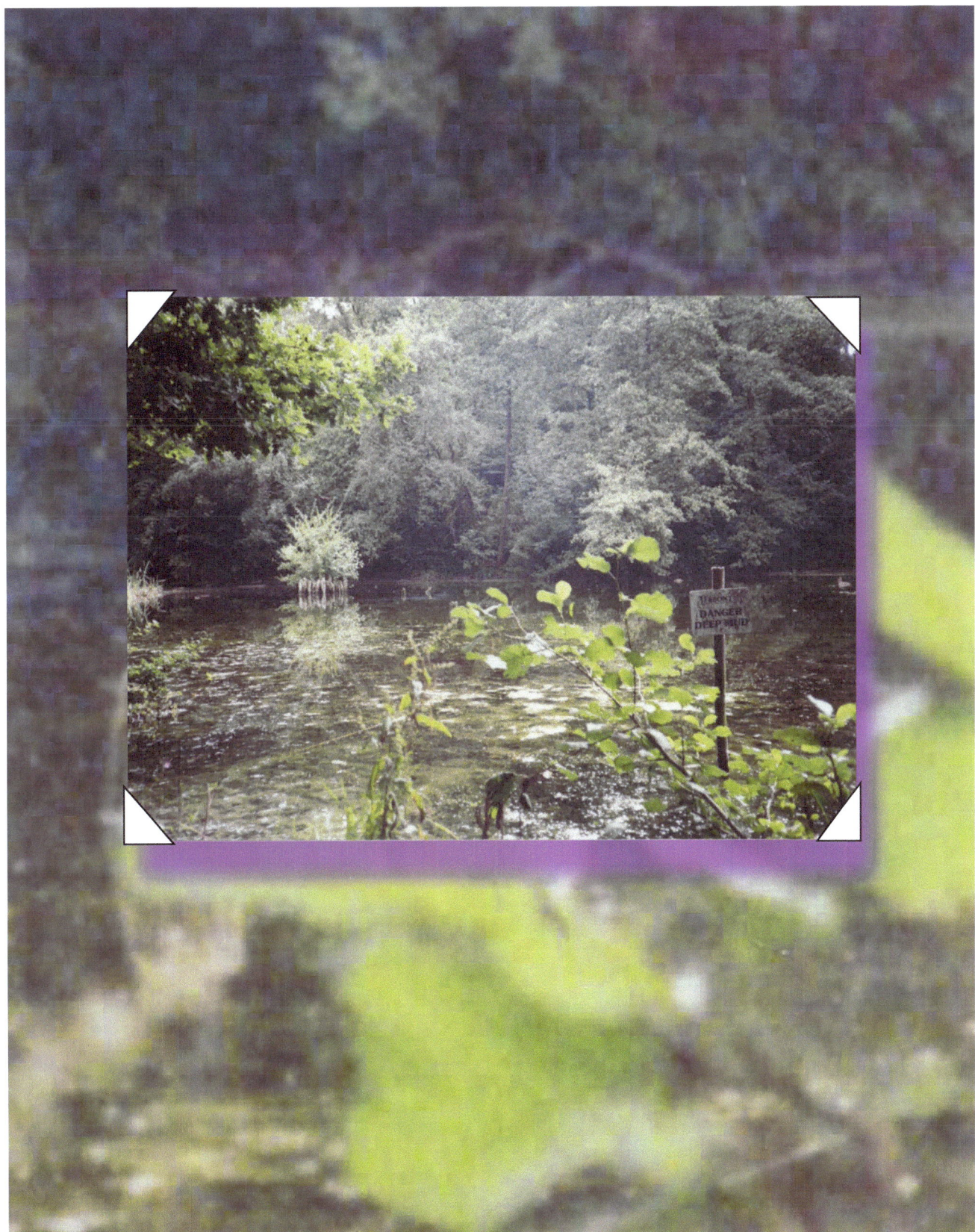

ARWEN

You can enjoy running through the woods on Shotover Hill and just acting "like a kid." The lush deep greens and dense soft textures make it an easy place to let imaginations run wild.

Upon close inspection of what appear to be ordinary humans, you may see something extraordinary. Can you detect the Elfen wings and the bow and arrow carried discretely on the back?

These magical creatures appear to be descendants of the beautiful Arwen, with the Elfen light in her eyes, who loved so deeply and faithfully for thirty years waiting for her beloved Aragonm.

--- Beauty, Mythic Romance ---

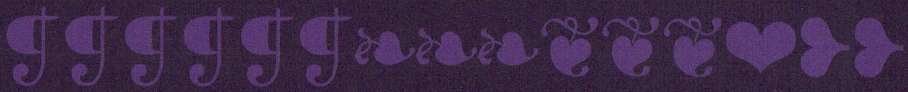

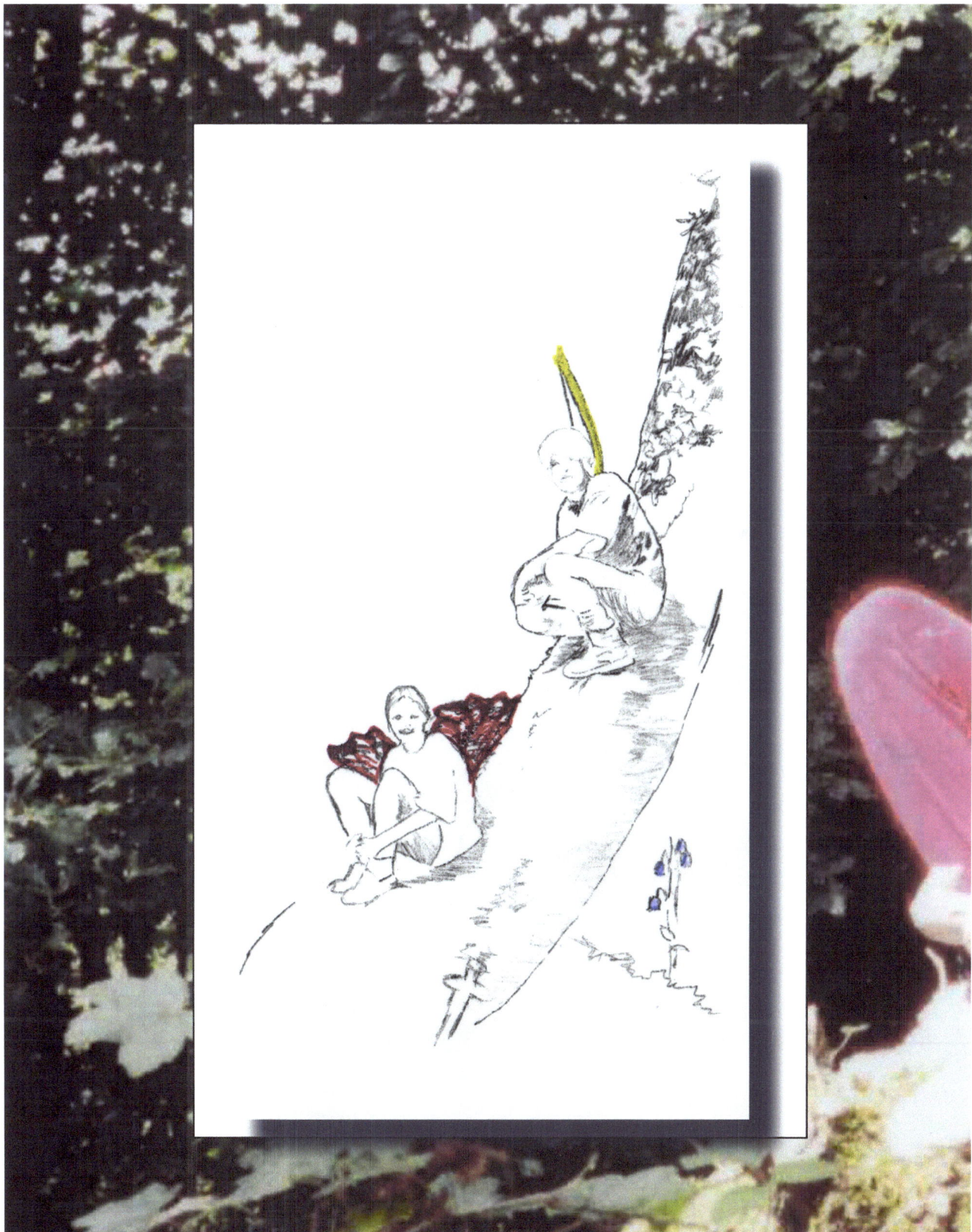

ARWEN

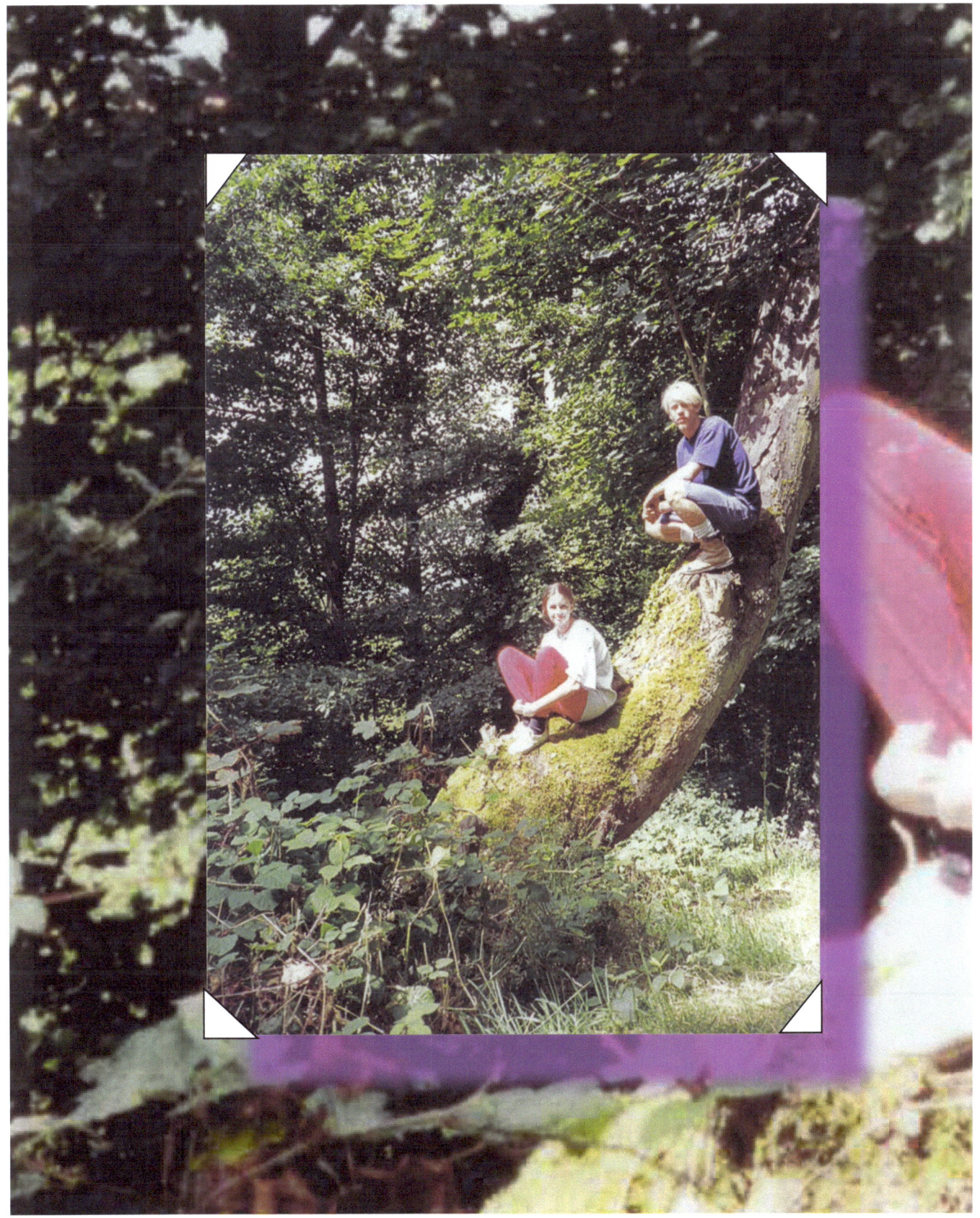

DWARFS

There is a beautiful shaded area with a broken-down brick wall and bench next to the pond in the nature reserve. Dwarves, who live sometimes to be as old as 250 years, seem to also find this a relaxing spot.

The wall was reconstructed and brought back to life by Marty, one of the volunteers on the "Kilns" renovation. He spent his last hours in Oxford before returning to the USA repairing this wall and bench.

In his late night repairs Marty probably didn't realize how much help he got. If you look closely, you may see a dwarf under the covering of the tree branches behind the wall holding one of his tools, and putting the final touches on the project.

---Transformation, Devotion ---

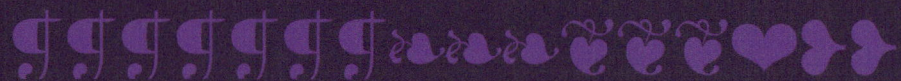

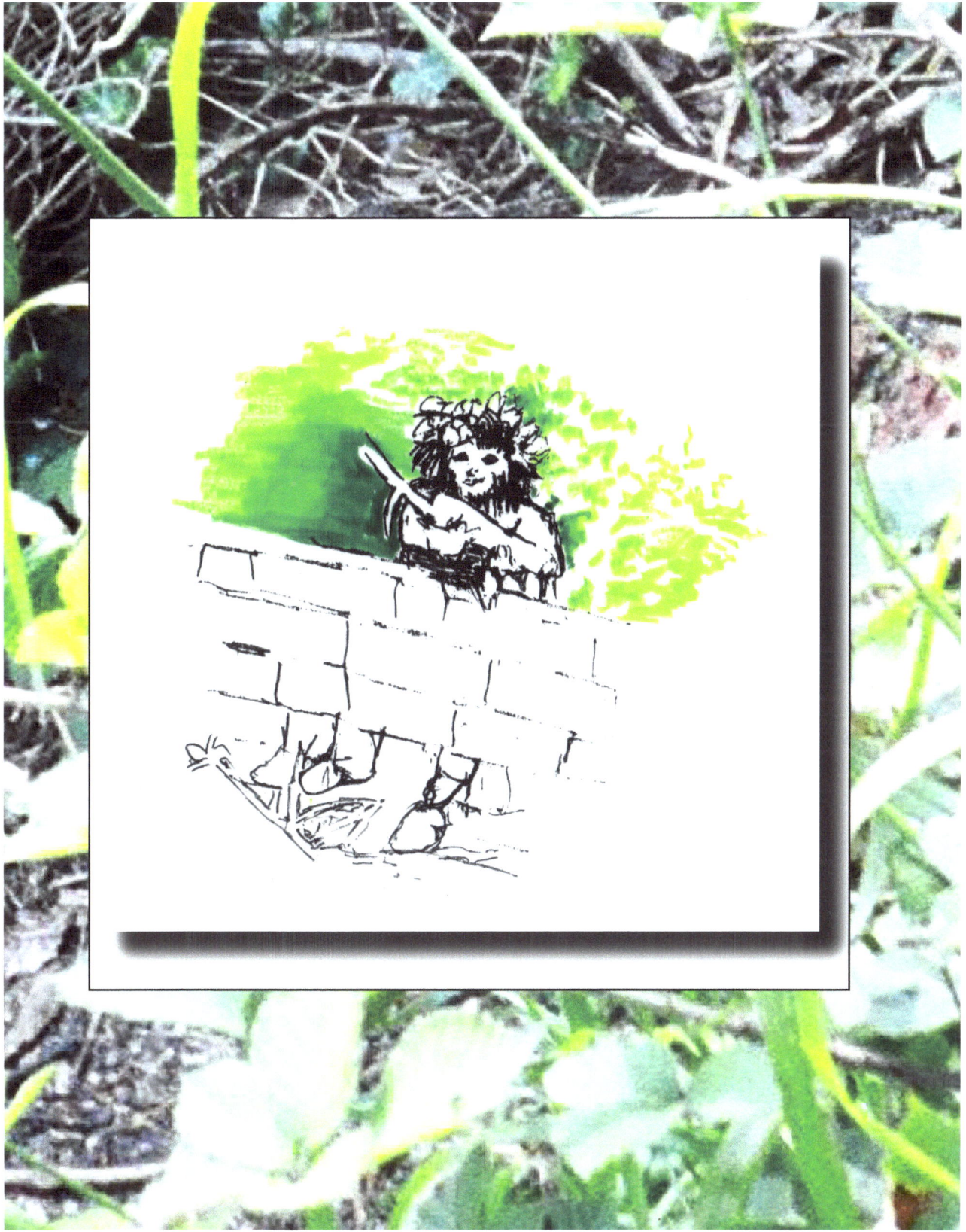

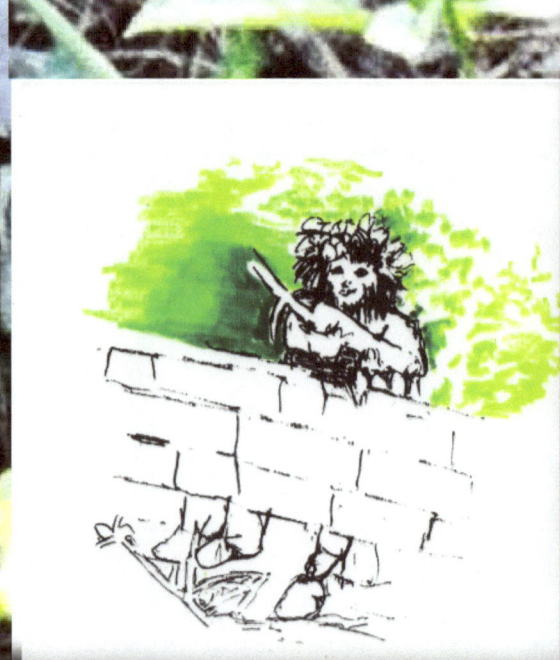

DWARFS

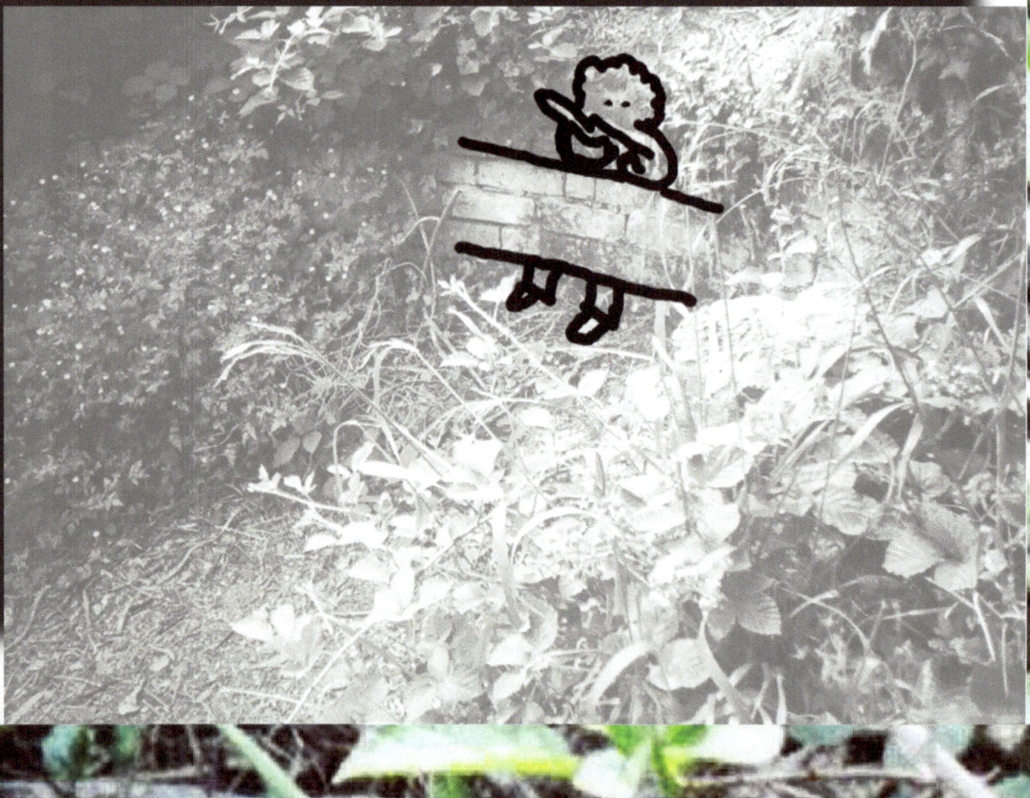

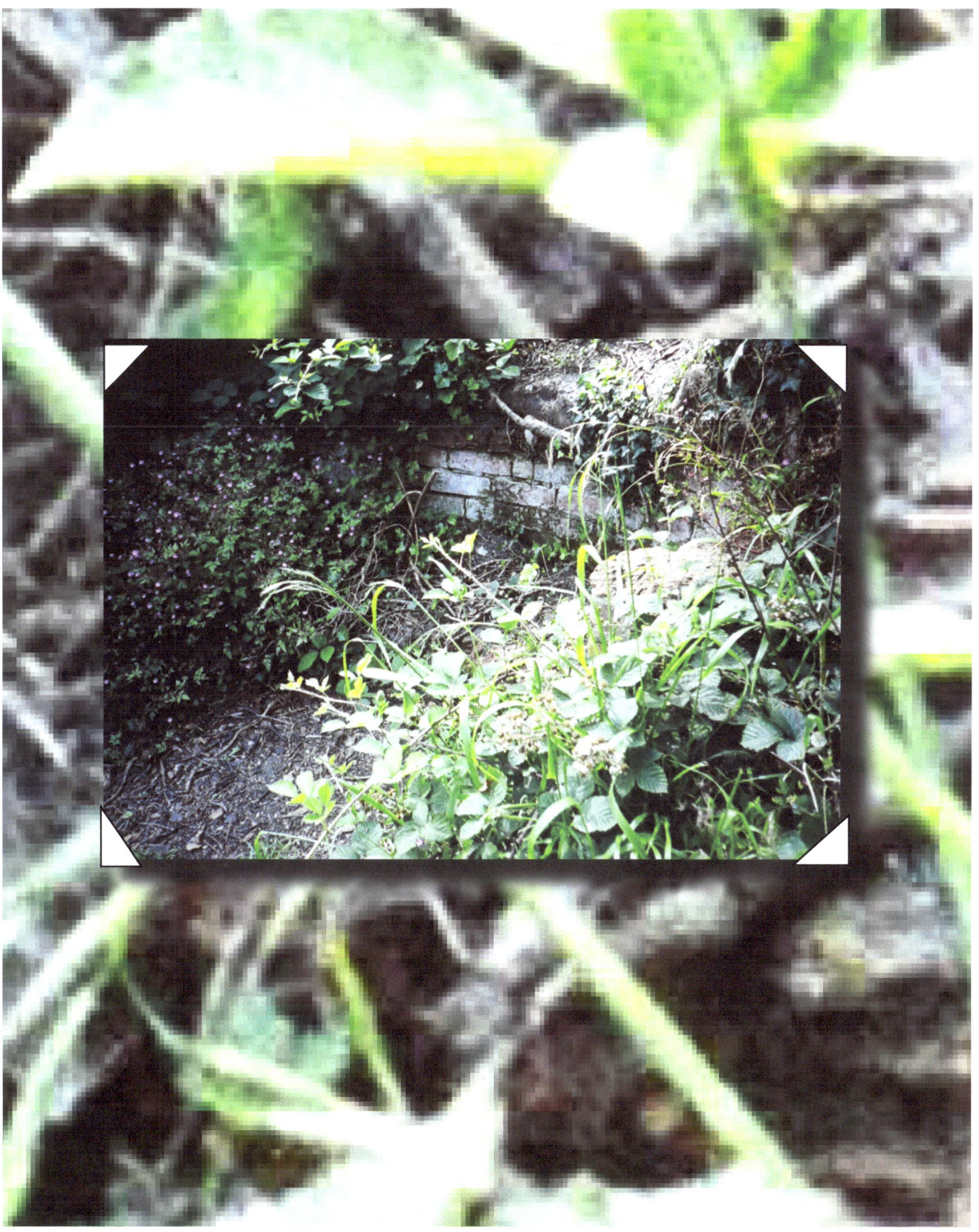

HOBBITS

The grass and the reeds have grown so tall that they form a sort of forest for little people In the reserve. If you took carefully, what a joyful sight it is to catch glimpses of Hobbits walking happily together through the clearing.

Hobbits have a particular way of being in the world, walking with a cheerful gait that makes a person glad just to be alive and be able to watch them.

Could this be be Frodo and Sam coming down the path right now.....?

--- Humility, Mercy, Perseverance ---

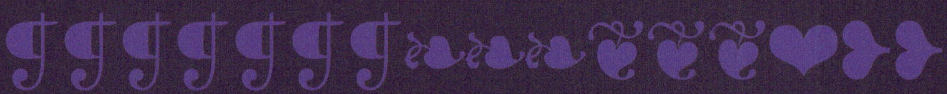

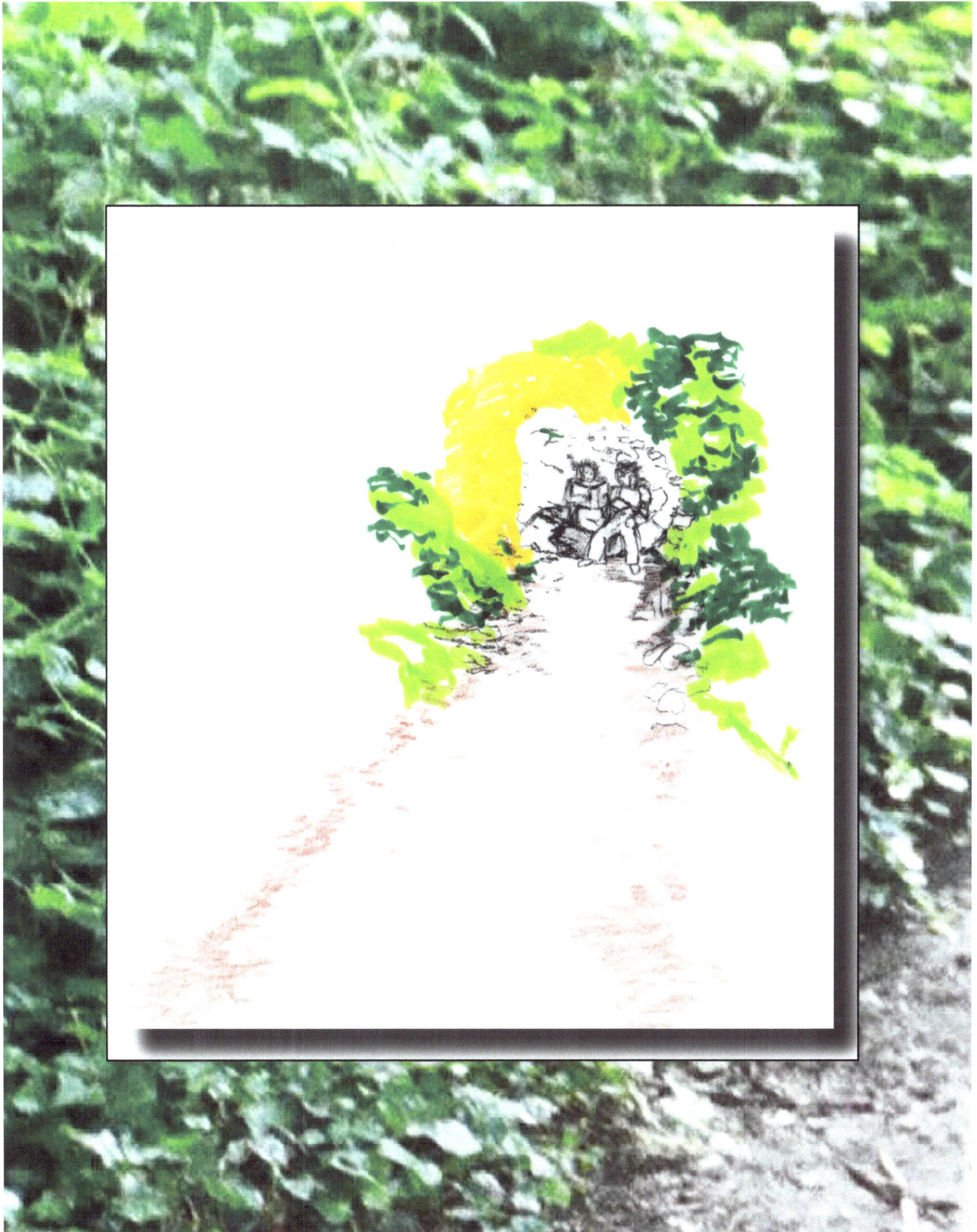

HOBBITS

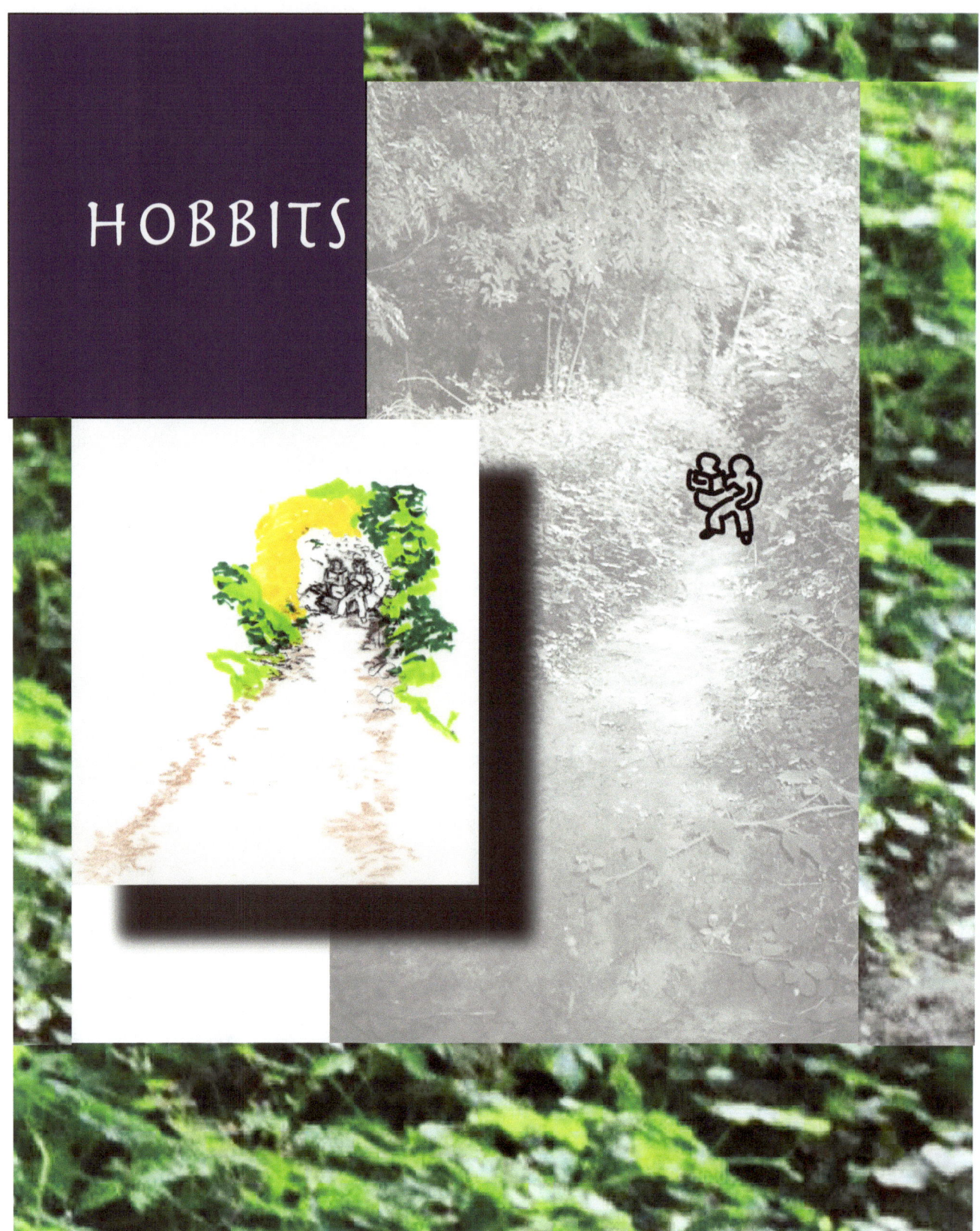

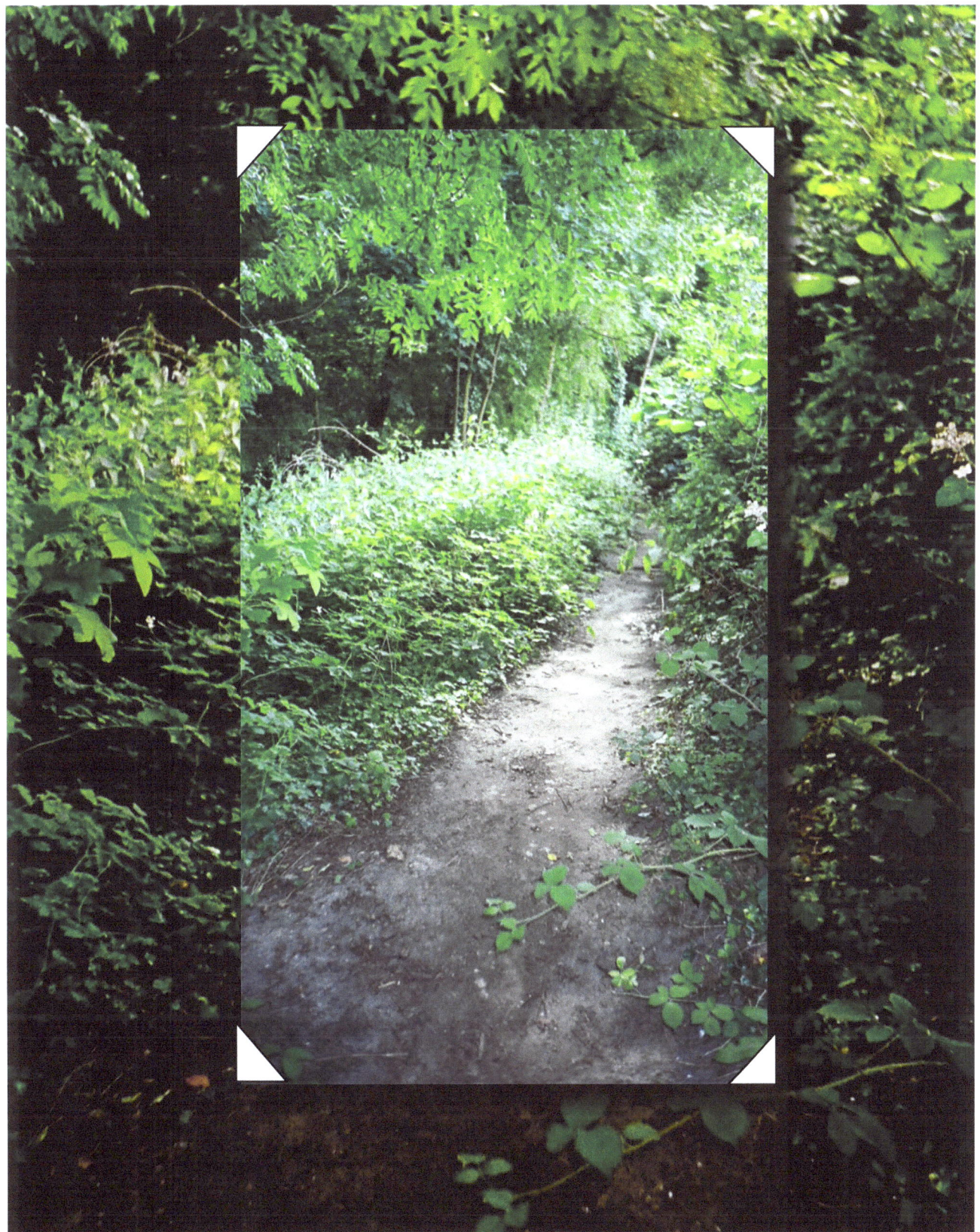

GANDALF

The trees surrounding the pond form a friendly blanket of green that wraps its arms around the area. They are a welcoming sight and always seem to provide a cheerful place of shelter for birds and animals.

Probably it should be no surprise to find someone else at home among the trees. You may not notice him at first, but his distinctive staff is the easiest identifying characteristic to spot. Focusing more closely, among the branches of the trees you can just make out his outline, and then find his long flowing beard and smiling face.

--- Wisdom, Helper, Friend ---

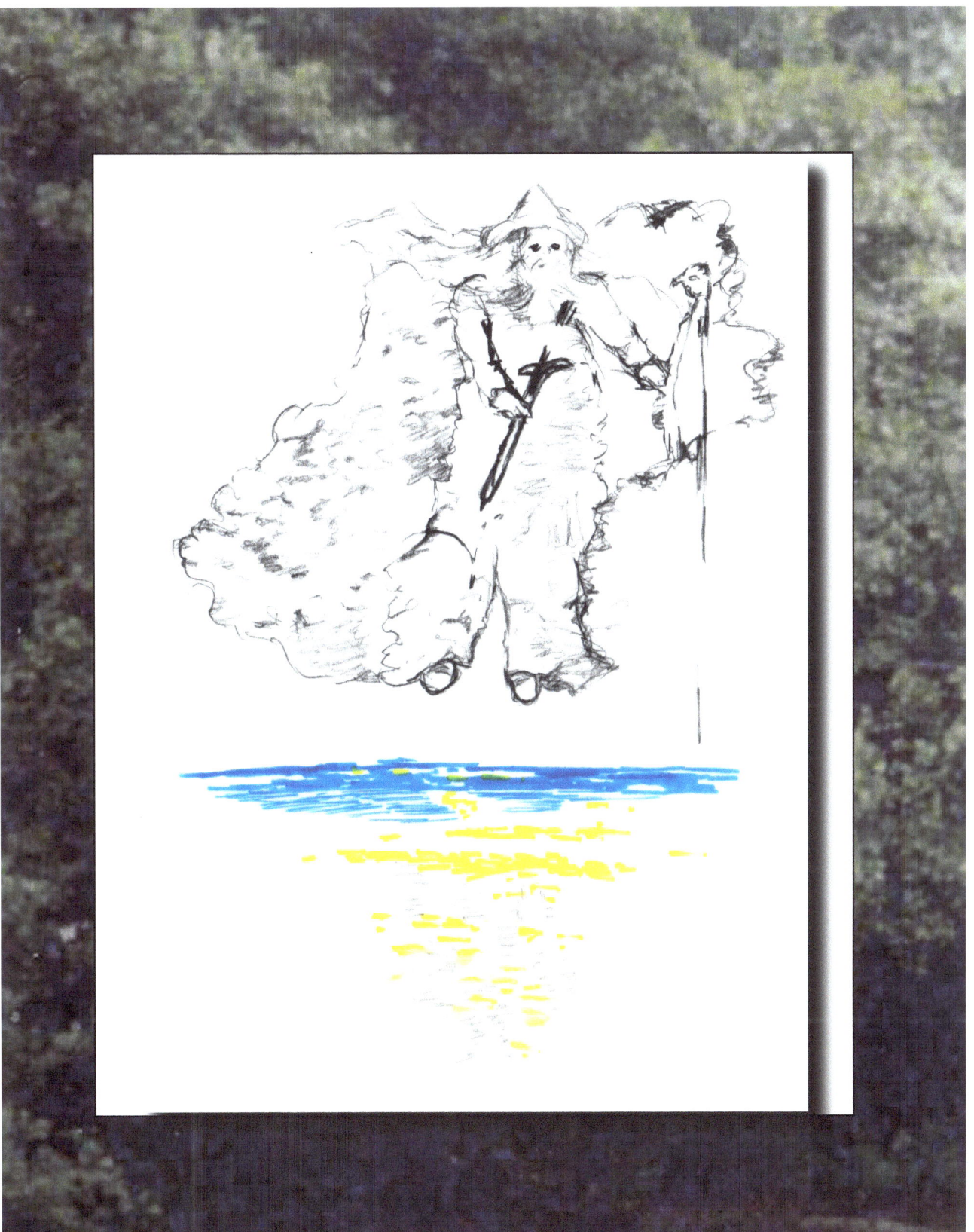

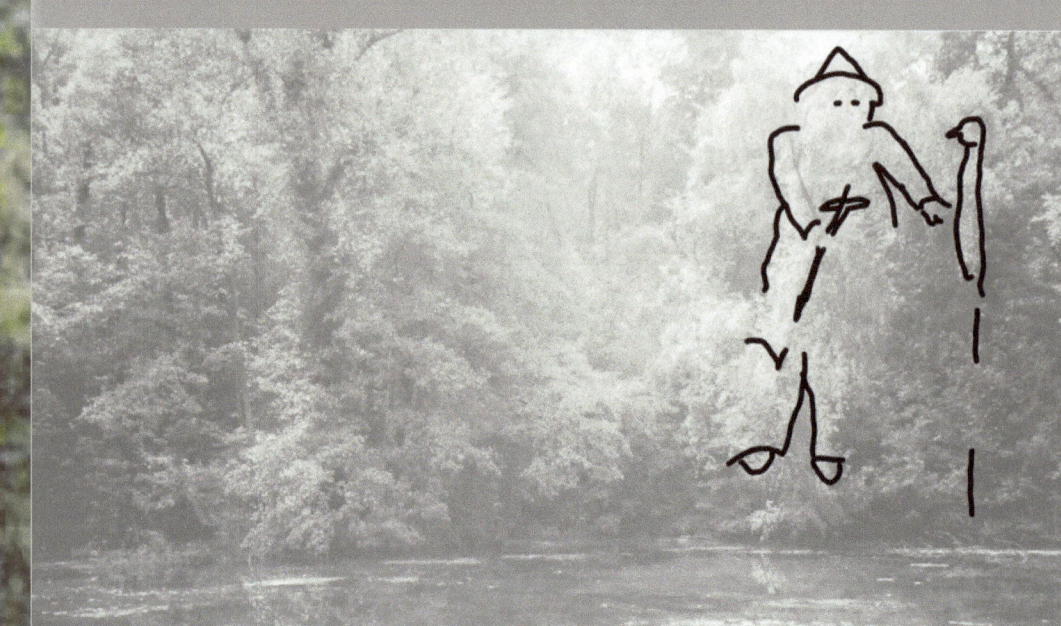

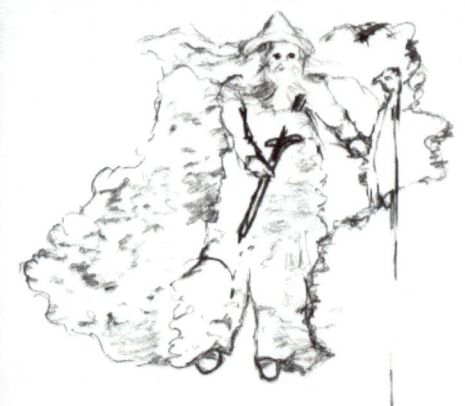

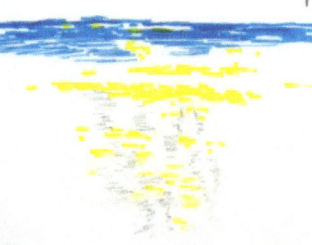

GANDALF

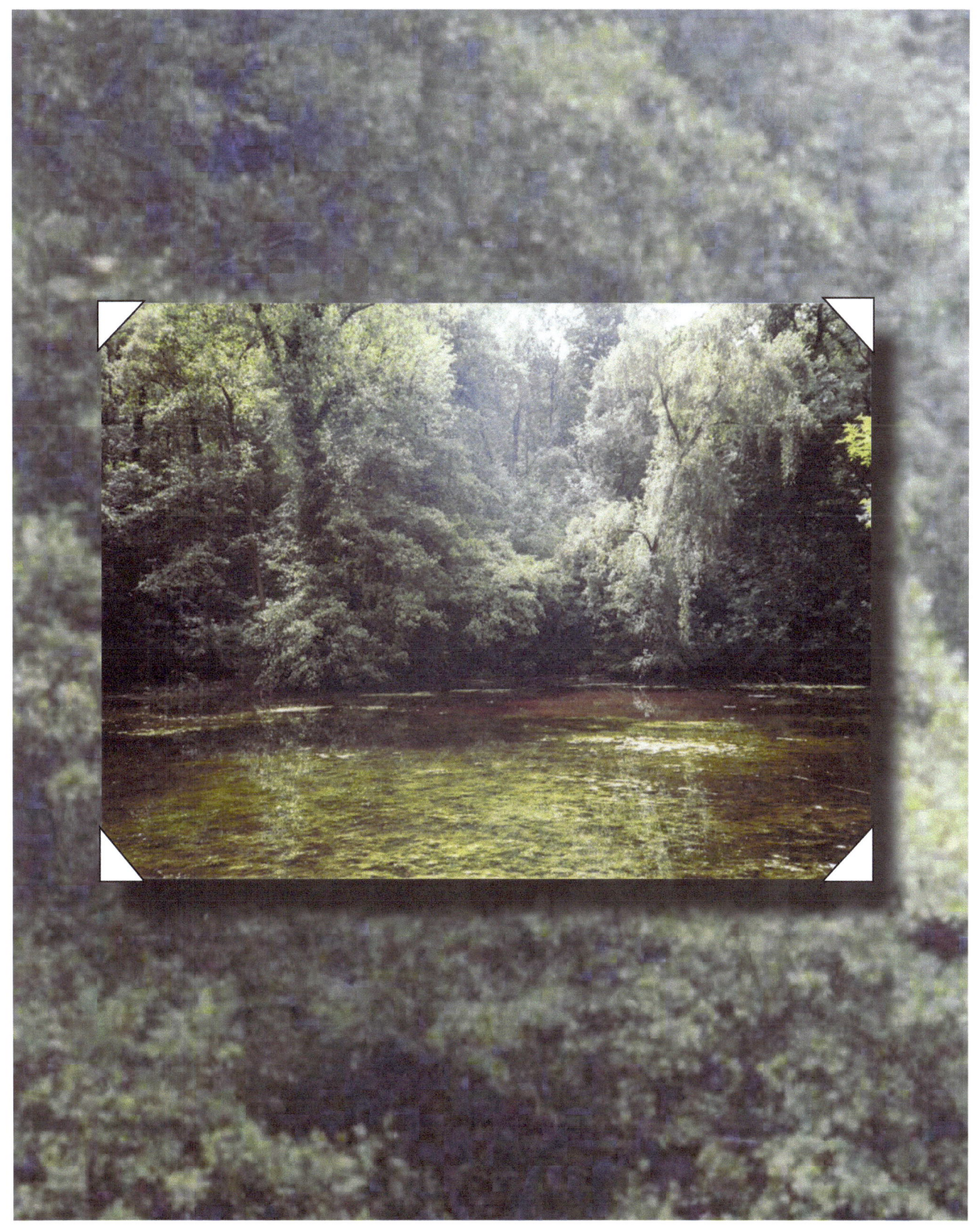

GOLDENBERRY

When you are "punting" along one of the streams that runs through Oxford and meanders around the colleges, you may have the opportunity to see River Maidens.

Elizabeth accidentally caught the first glimpse of Goldenberry and one other River Maiden. Elizabeth was courageously trying her hand at maneuvering a punt through the water. Standing precariously on the front end of the craft and pushing an extraordinarily long pole into the mud at the bottom of the stream, Elizabeth felt her sunglasses slip off her nose and into the water. She dropped to her knees to see the glasses slowly sinking to the bottom.

From that vantage point, she looked along the riverbank and, to her utter amazement shouted, " I see beautiful maidens with golden hair streaming out behind their backs! They're picking flowers along the banks of the stream!"

--- Unfallen woman ---

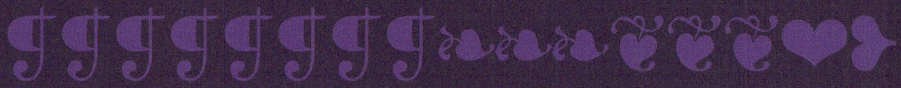

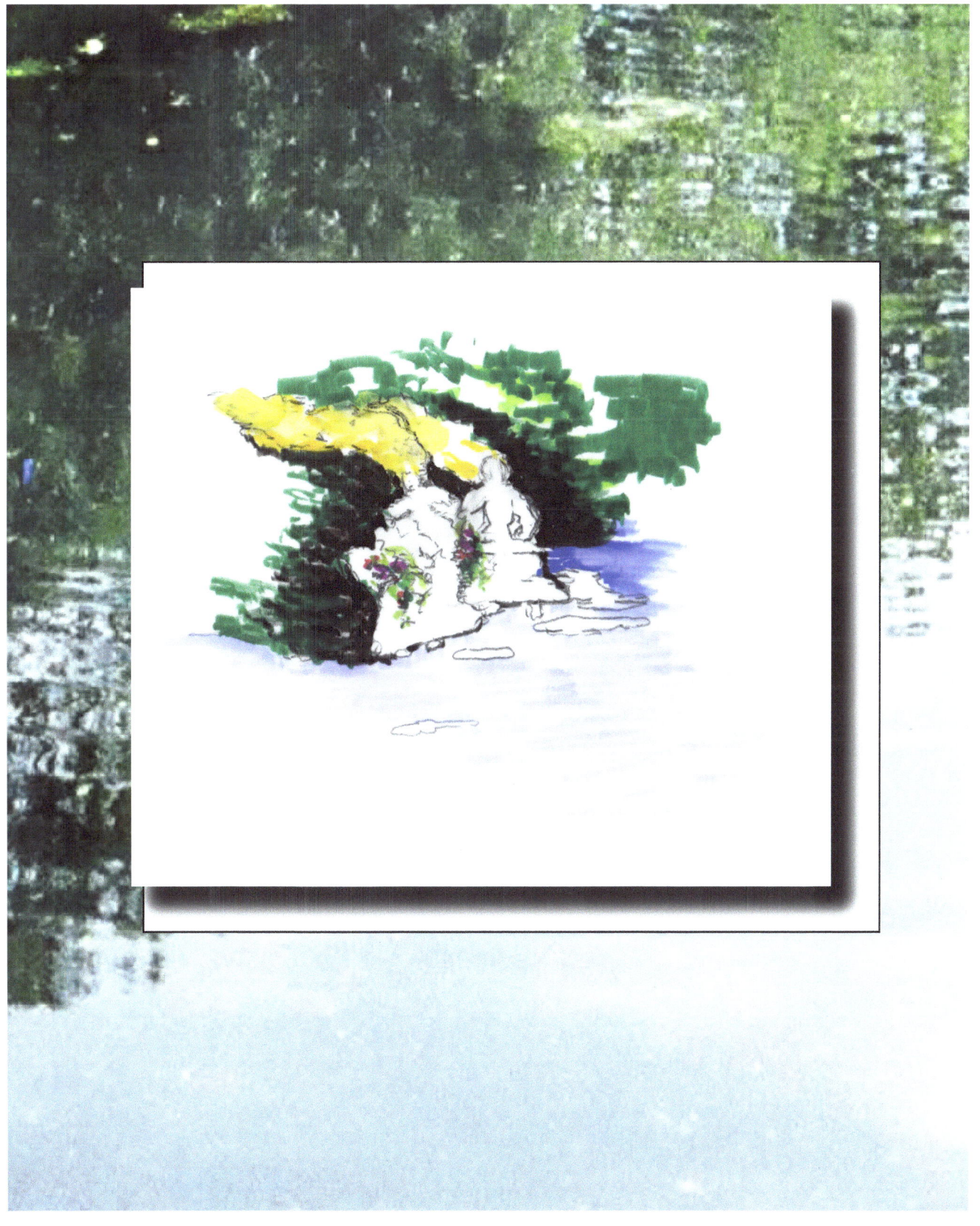

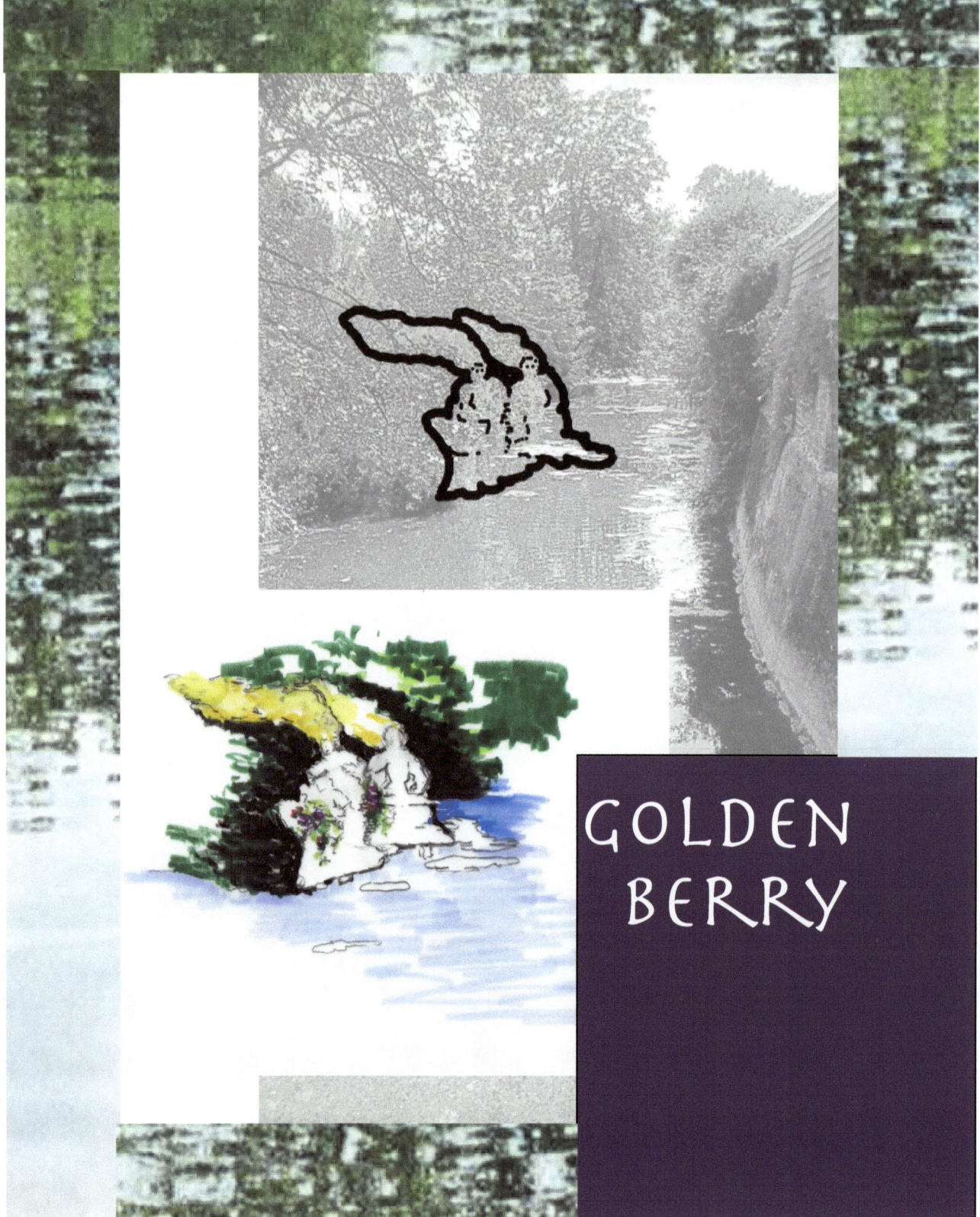

GOLDEN
BERRY

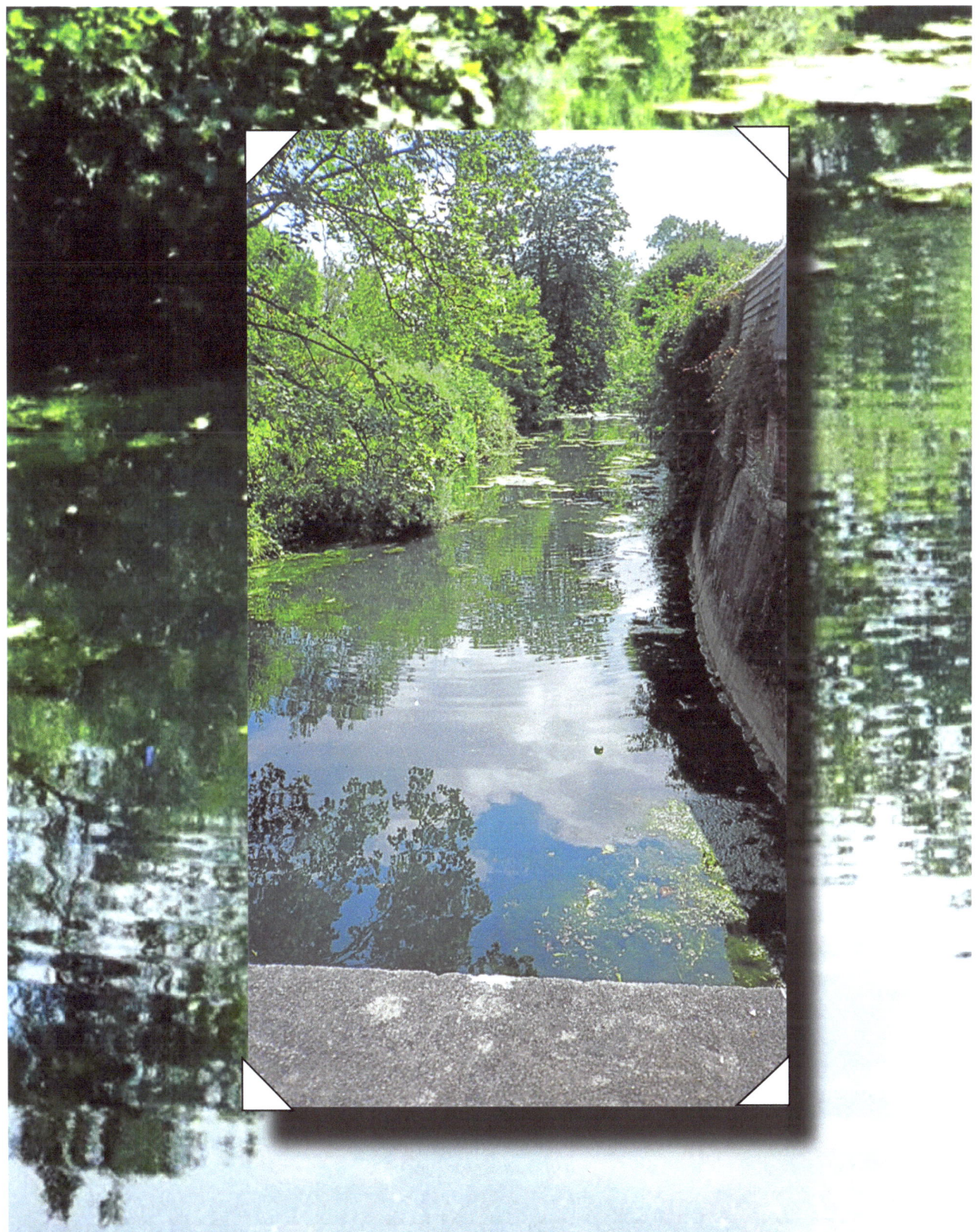

TOM BOMBADIL

The woods of Oxford are reminiscent of Lothlorien in the *Lord of the Rings* where you can easily feel the enchantment shared by elves and fairies.

If you are very fortunate, you may be able to listen intently and hear a nonsense song that sounds like, "Hey doll Merry doll King a dong dilo... Fal la! The willow." If you do hear the singing then look carefully through any clearing in the woods for a pair of yellow boots and a blue feather bobbing just above the bushes. You will not be dreaming, for you may have just spotted the merry and blithe Tom Bombadil who is known for having such great power, knowledge and joy.

-- Unfallen man ---

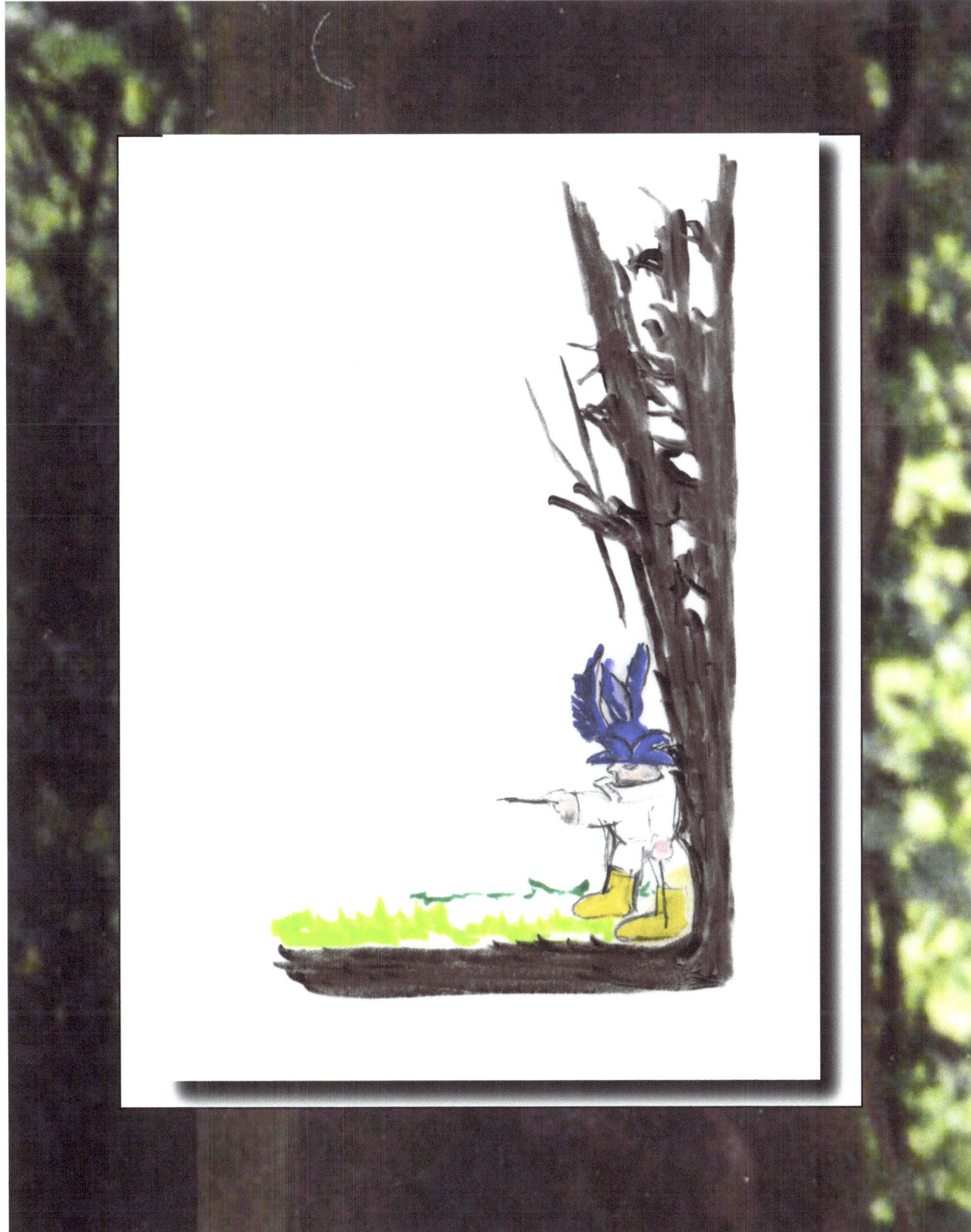

TOM BOMBADIL

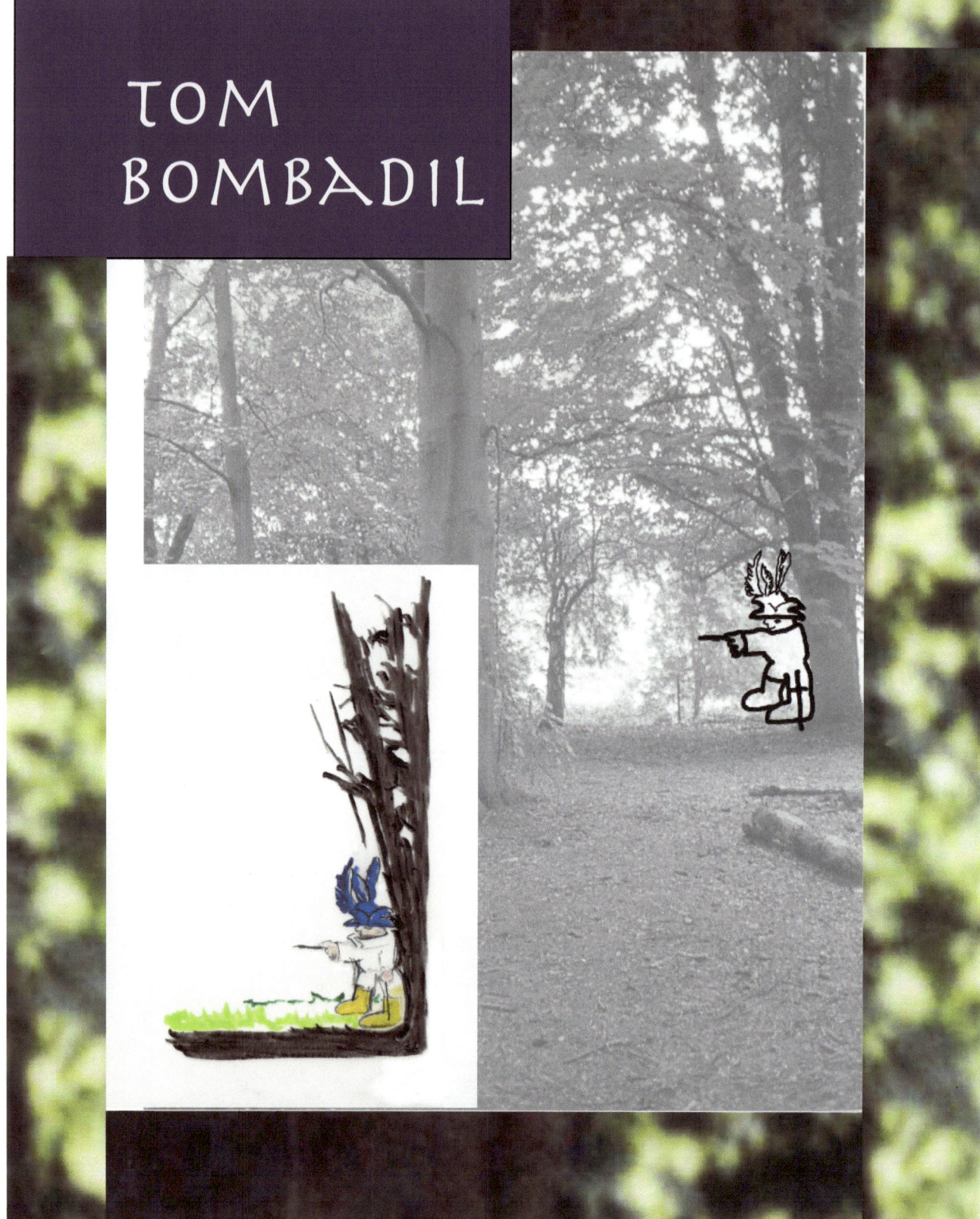

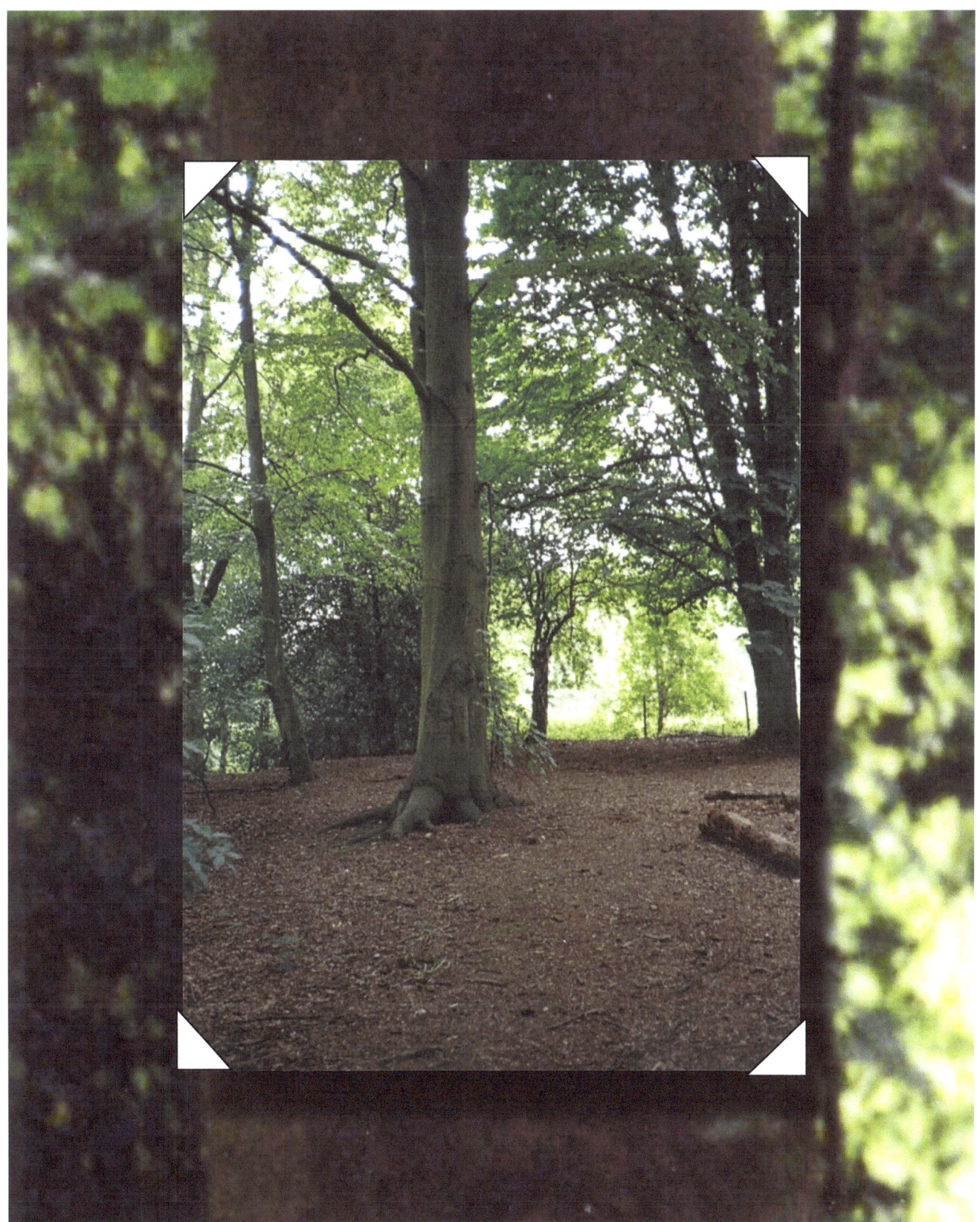

TALKING BEASTS

In Narnia there were many talking beasts in the olden times. We have read about Mr and Mrs Beaver and who could ever forget Reepicheep?

In our day we might not be expecting to come across talking beasts but they are still with us: now they seem just a little less inclined to talk and communicate with our race since many have lost their imagination.

As you are becoming more in touch with your senses you might take the time to look into the eyes of a four legged friend. By carefully listening you may hear "I wuv you, I wuv you,....."

--- Unconditional love ---

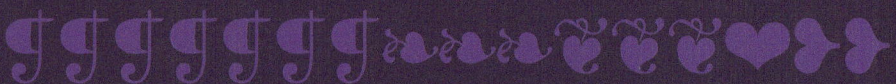

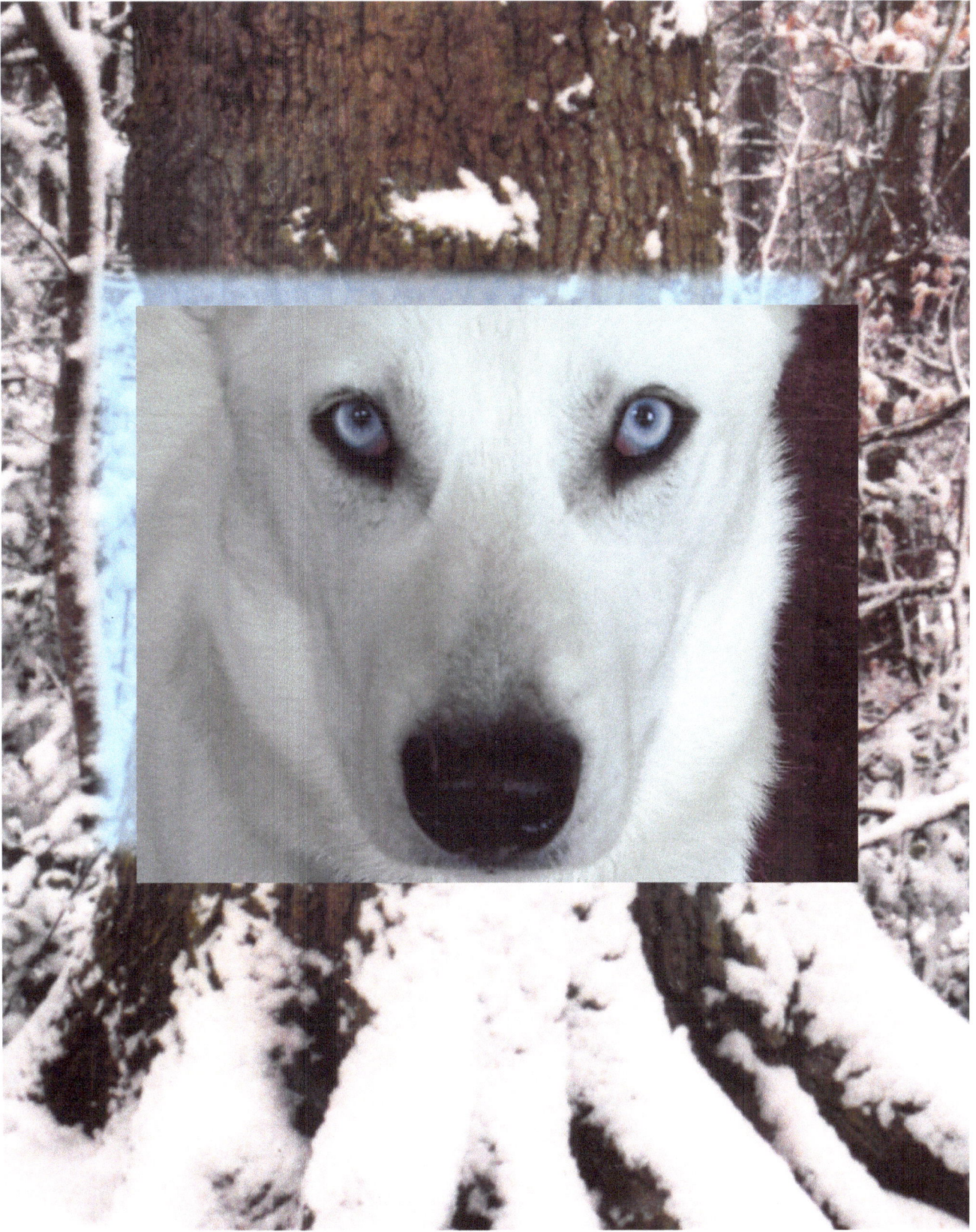

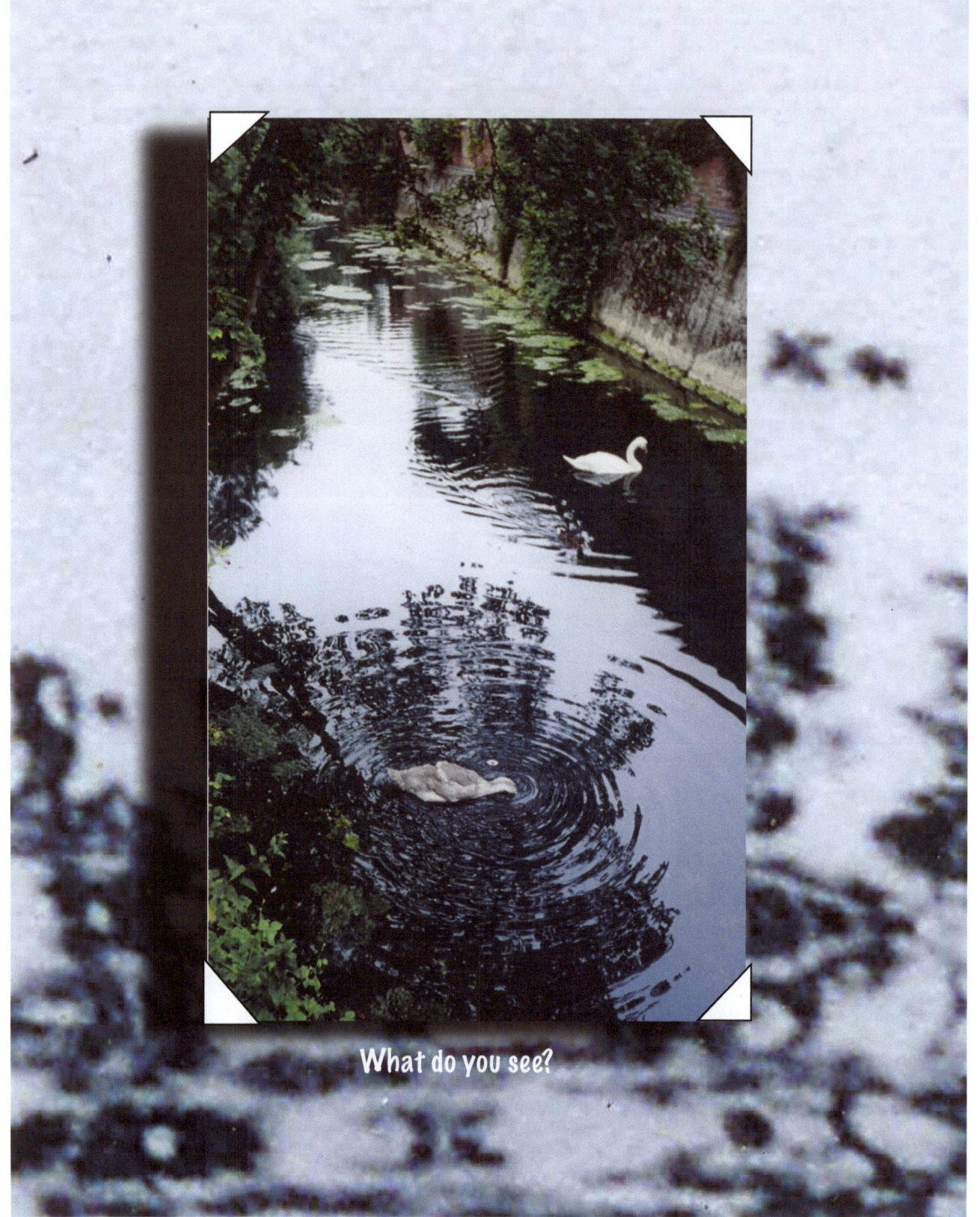

What do you see?

BAD GUYS

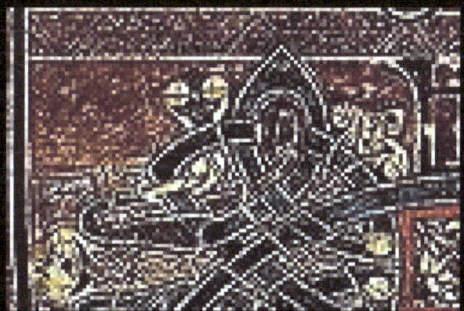

Book of Kells illustration Circa 800 (public domain)

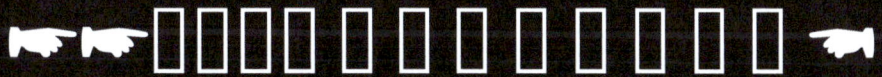

SARUMAN

The back portion of St. Aldades Cemetery in downtown Oxford is an eerie place. There are tall trees and overgrown underbrush with skewed gravestones scattered about. Charles Williams is buried in St Aldades. Williams was an author and colleague of C.S Lewis and J.R.R. Tolkien and was also a member of the Inklings literary group.

We visited St. Aldades at dusk and felt like a character in one of William's other worldly adventure novels. As Jenny leaned down to read the famous inscription on William's grave "Under His great mercy" darkened by the shadow of a great evergreen tree, a bird swooped down and grazed the hair on the top of her head! Rushing for the exit, screaming and wondering if this might be a message from a parallel universe, she saw a figure outlined in the vegetation behind the rows of tombstones - unmistakably it was Saruman.

--- Disgraced, Corrupted power --

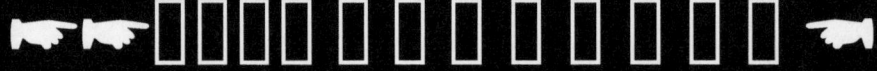

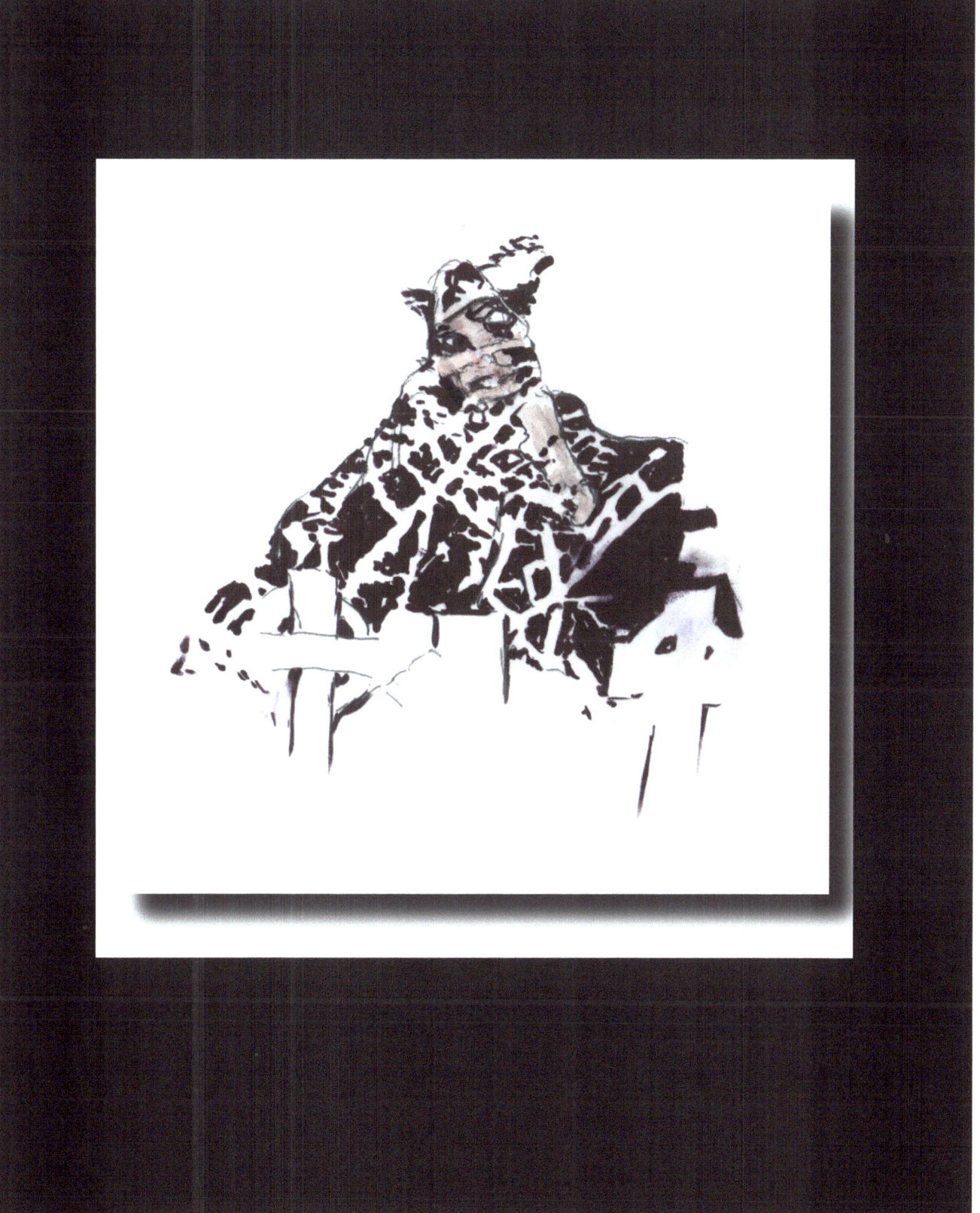

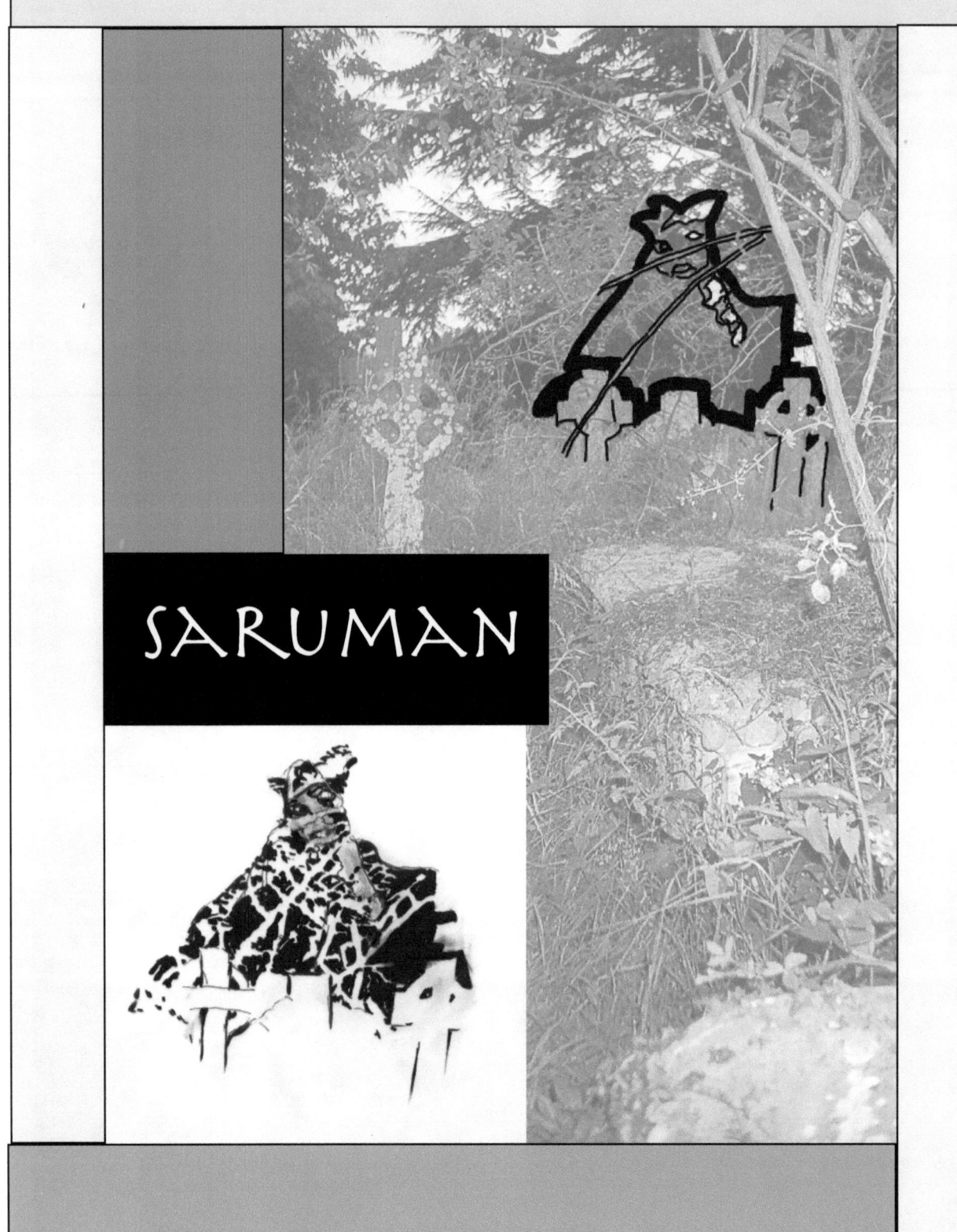

SARUMAN

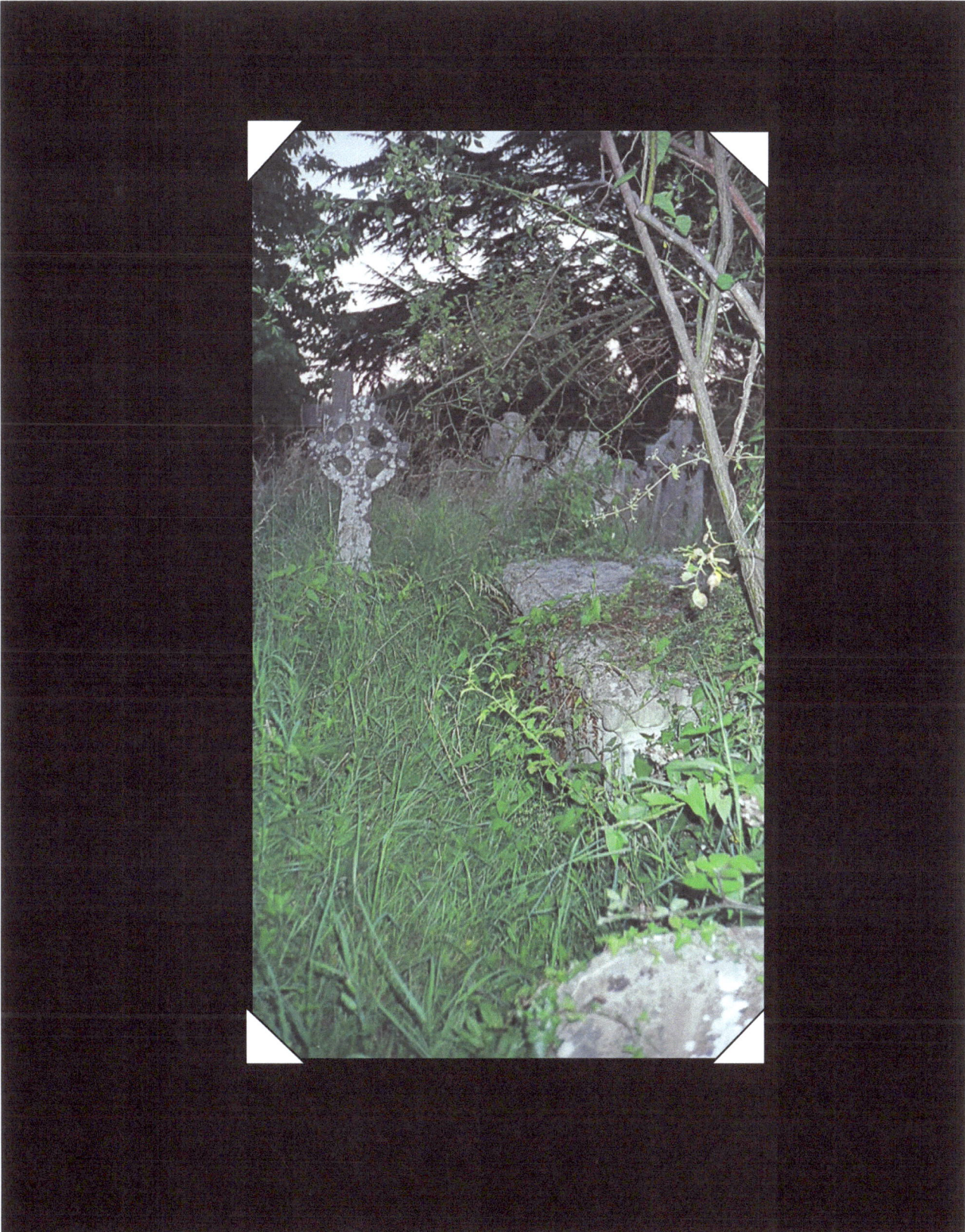

NAZGUL

Even in broad daylight St. Aldades Cemetery in downtown Oxford seems to be an "Inhabited" place The overgrown trees, long untended grass and tipping tombstones are foreboding.

We were just kidding around one day when Ernie decided to ran into the cemetery to take a quick photograph. He shouted, "Come and get me if I don't return!"

Once he reached the back of the cemetery where it merges with the forest, he had the uncomfortable feeling that he was not alone. Sensing movement on the bushes, he remained bravely on target with the mission of taking photos and getting out of the cemetery quickly!

When the noise of a horse whinnying drew Ernie's attention, he gasped in horror as he saw Nazgul -- invisible to the eyes, but defined by their black clothing outlined in the trees behind the tombstones.

--- Greedy, Temporary immortality --

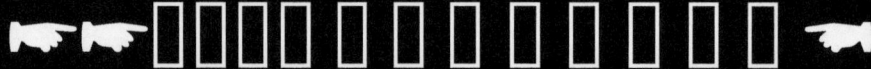

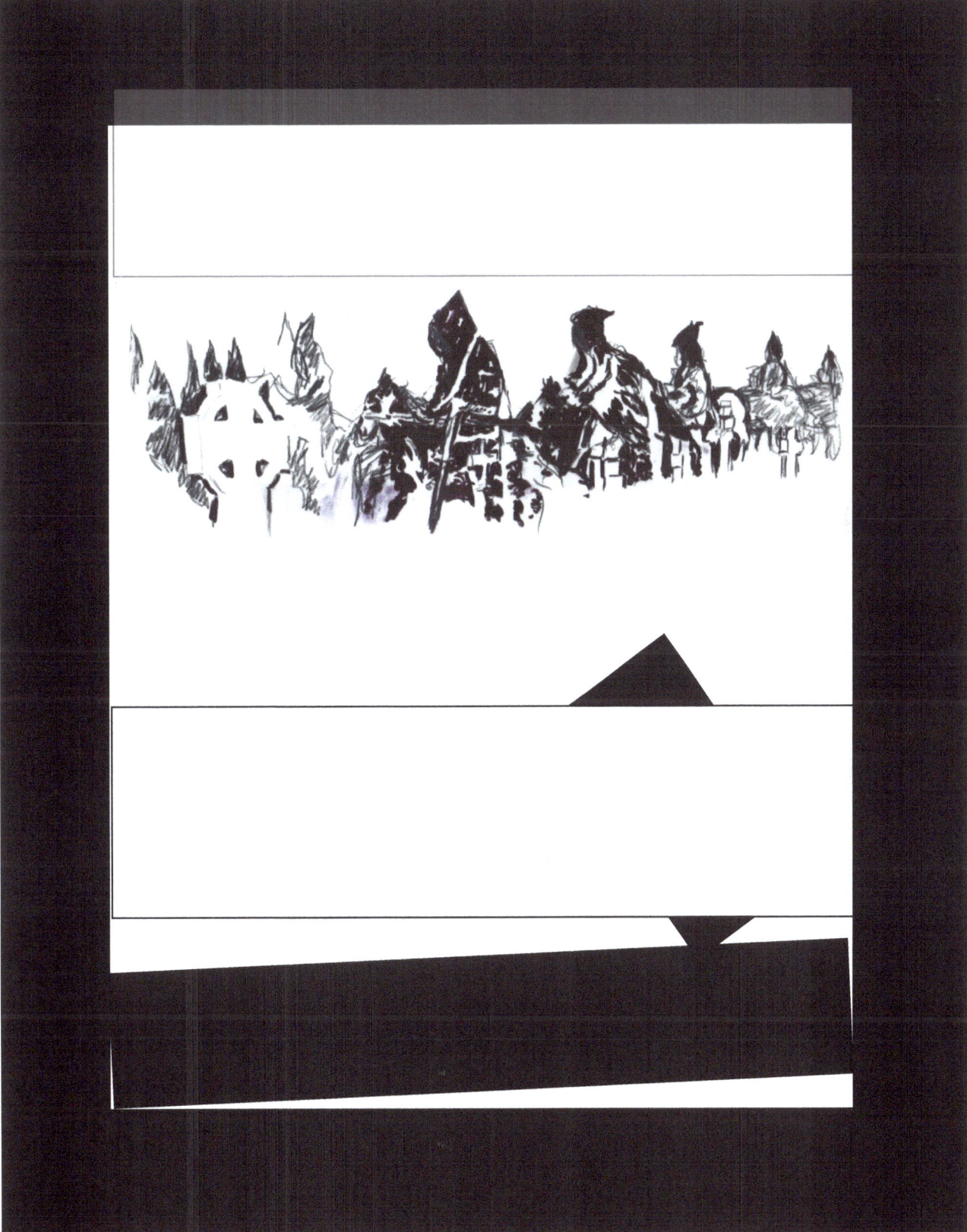

NAZGUL

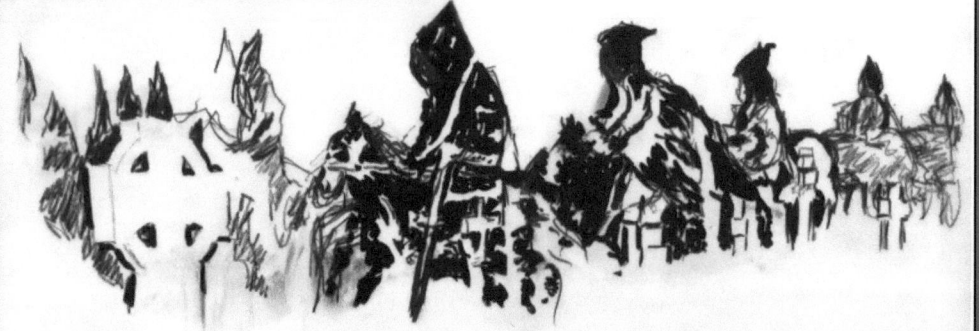

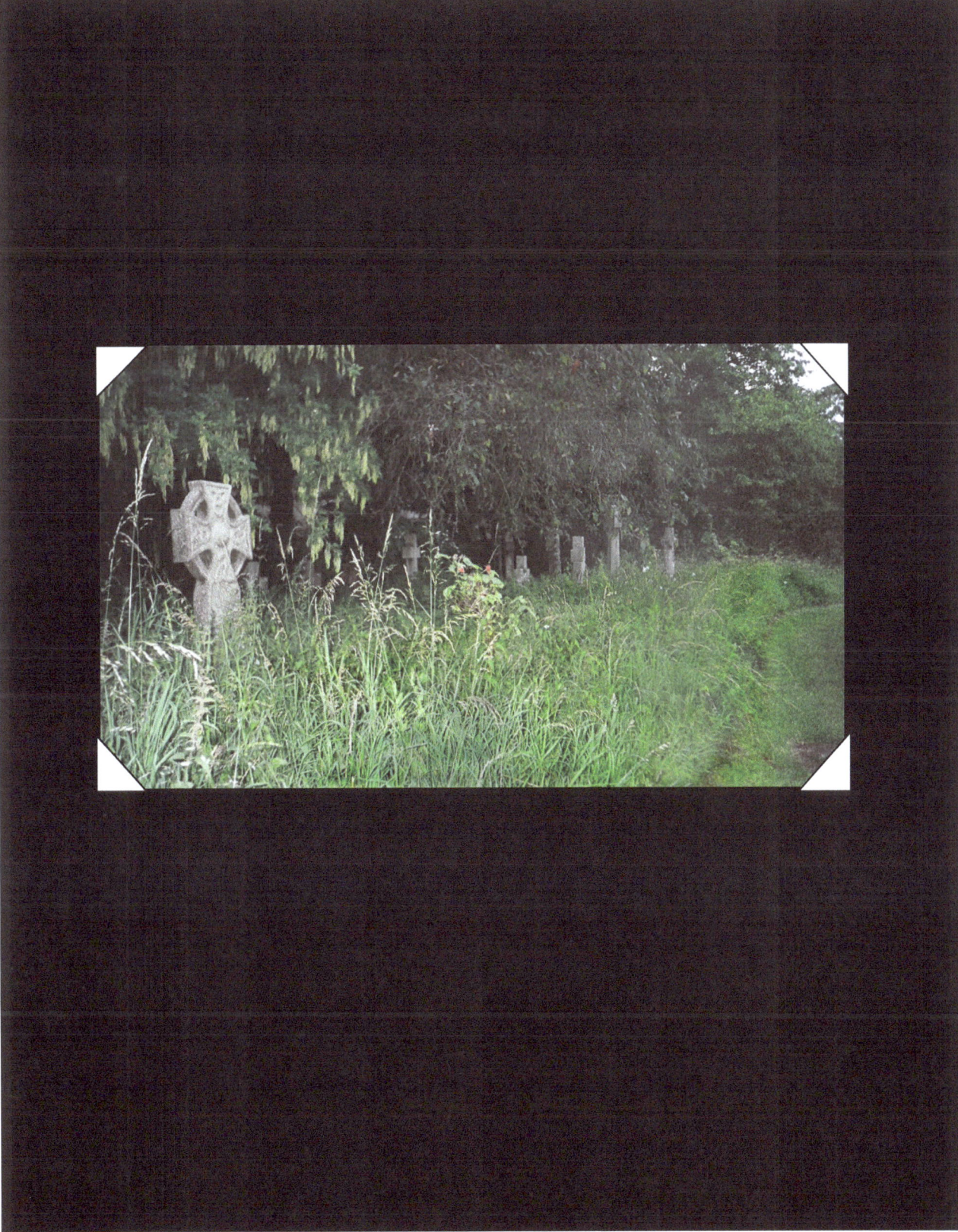

ORCS

A large tree grows next to the pond in the nature reserve in an eerie section of the woods in the nature reserve. The tree is adjacent to the railing and its roots extend Into the pond and across the path.

One fateful day, Susan was walking hurriedly along that section of the path when she tripped and fell face down. Of all places, this was the worst place to find herself -- defenseless against her imagination and surrounded by creepy vibes.

As Susan gingerly lifted her head and peeked out at what was around her, she had a horrible revelation and shouted out that the "root that had tripped me was in fact not a root! This is the limb of an Orc -- not the limb of a tree!" This unholy place was nothing less than an Orc breading ground where evil forces caused Orcs to rise from the ground and join forces against the Fellowship of the Ring..

--- Soulless, Evil, Fallen creatures ---

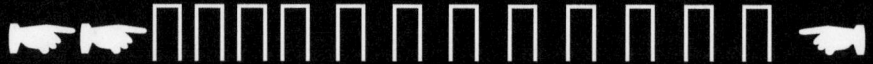

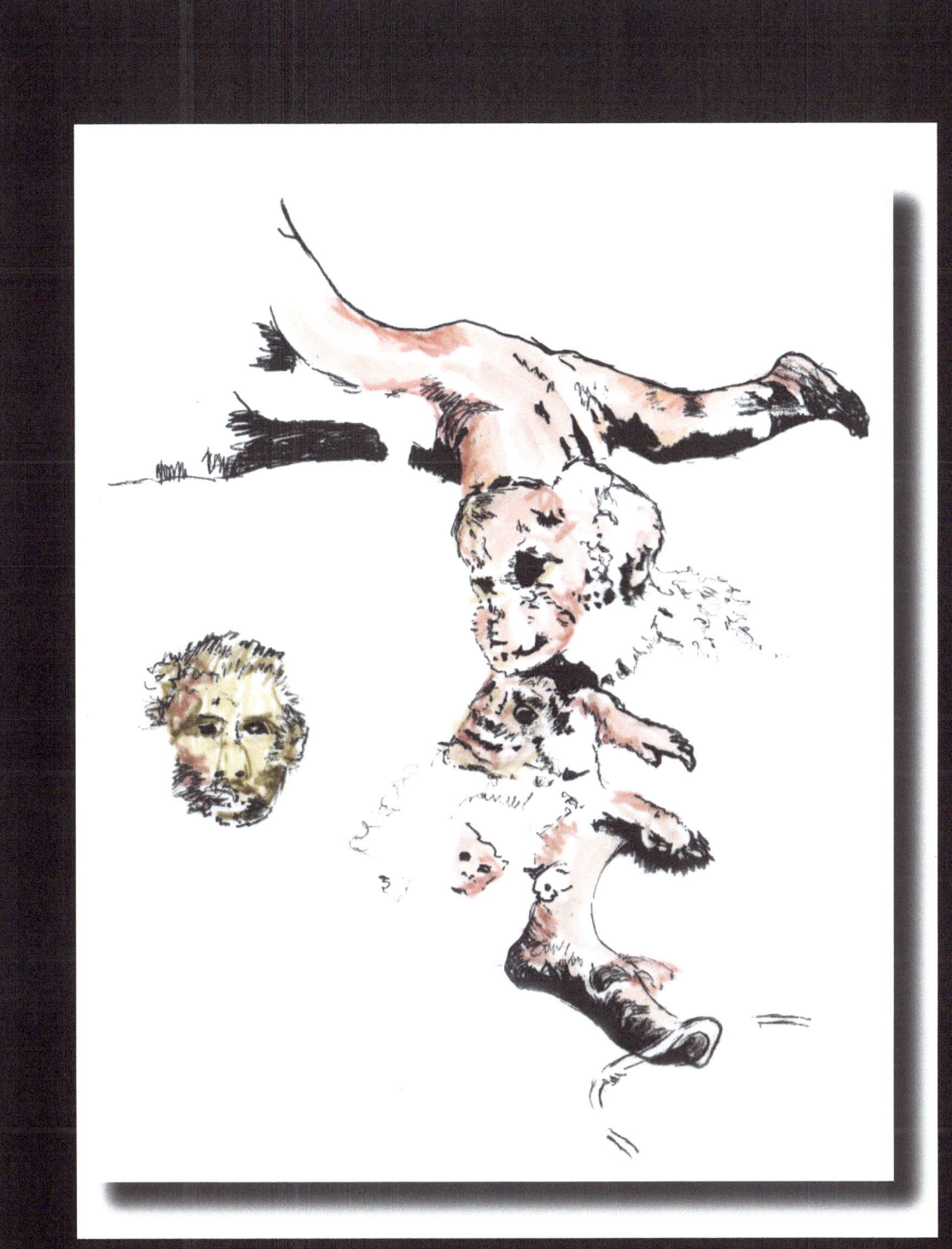

ORCS

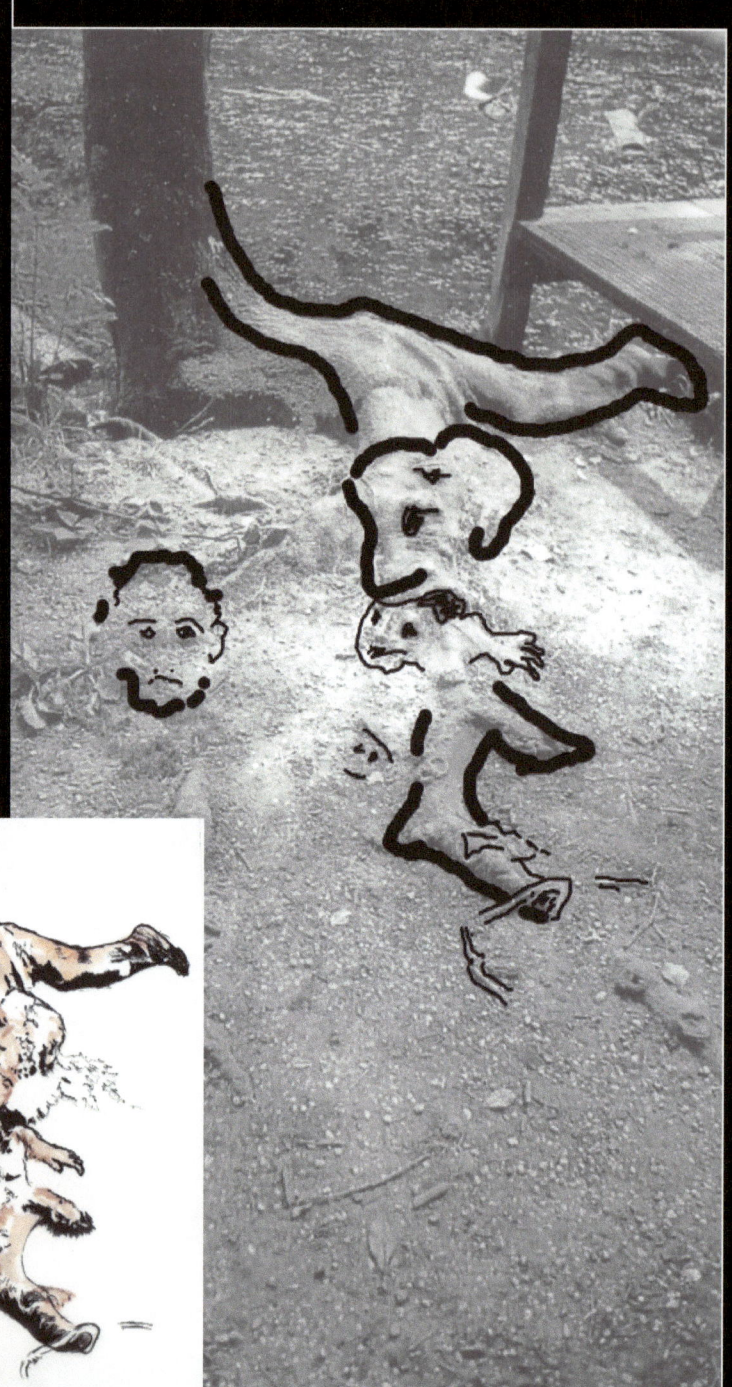

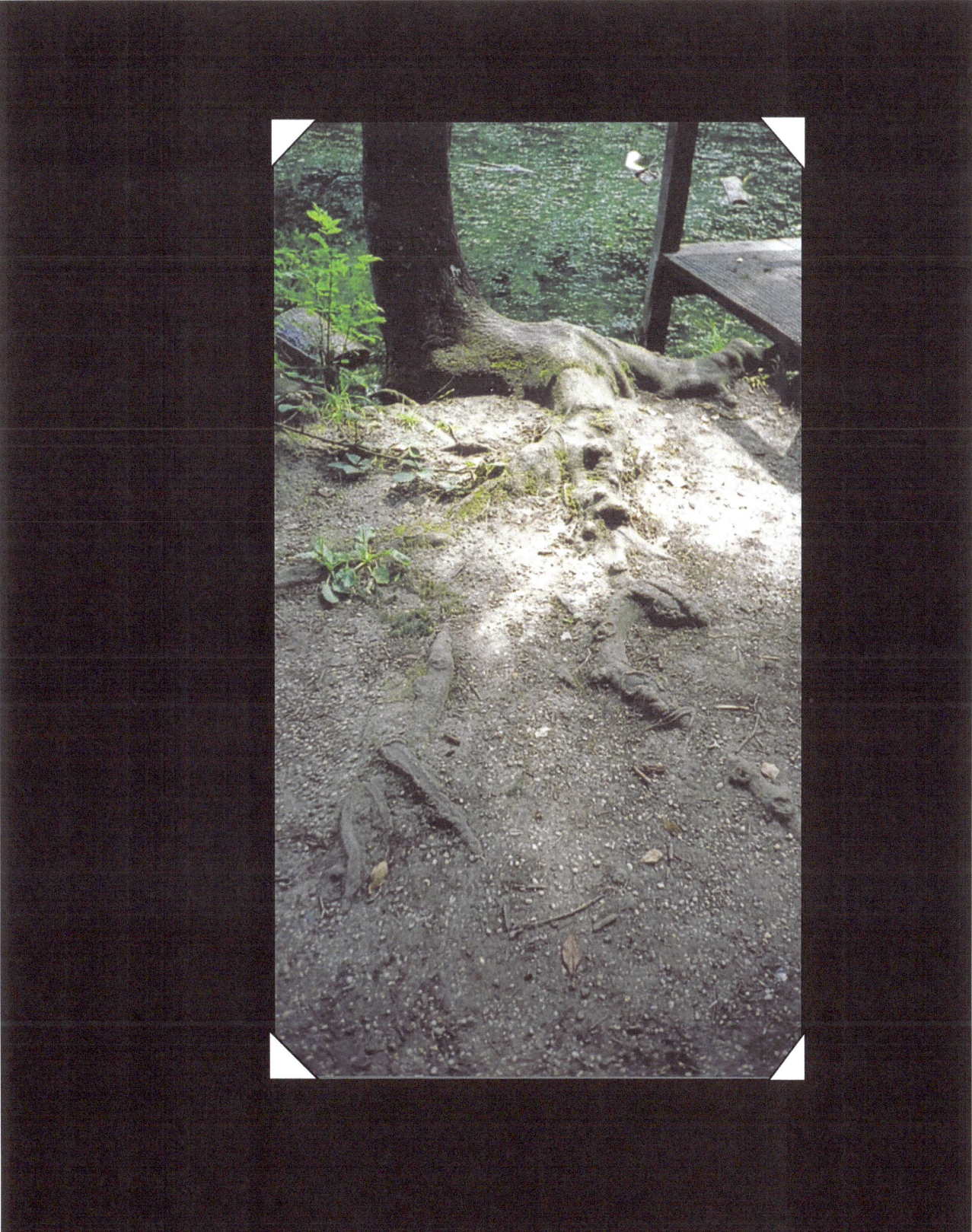

URU-HAI ORCS

There is a most peculiar plant that grows in a particular section of the woods on Shotover Hill. The leaves are large and tough and the plant produces a tall stalk with blood red berries hanging along the steam. There Is a foreboding atmosphere about this place and we usually walked around it.

Word has it that some brave soul ventured into that area and saw a heinous sight. Uruk-hai-orcs are not weakened by the sun like other orcas and one boldly showed this face. His head was shaded by a huge leaf, his ax weapon was held high and from his mouth dripped either bright red blood or the juice of some of the berries.

--- Mark of the beast, Violent ---

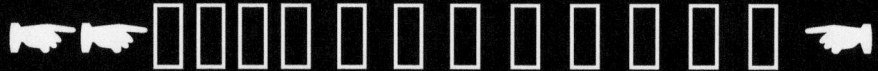

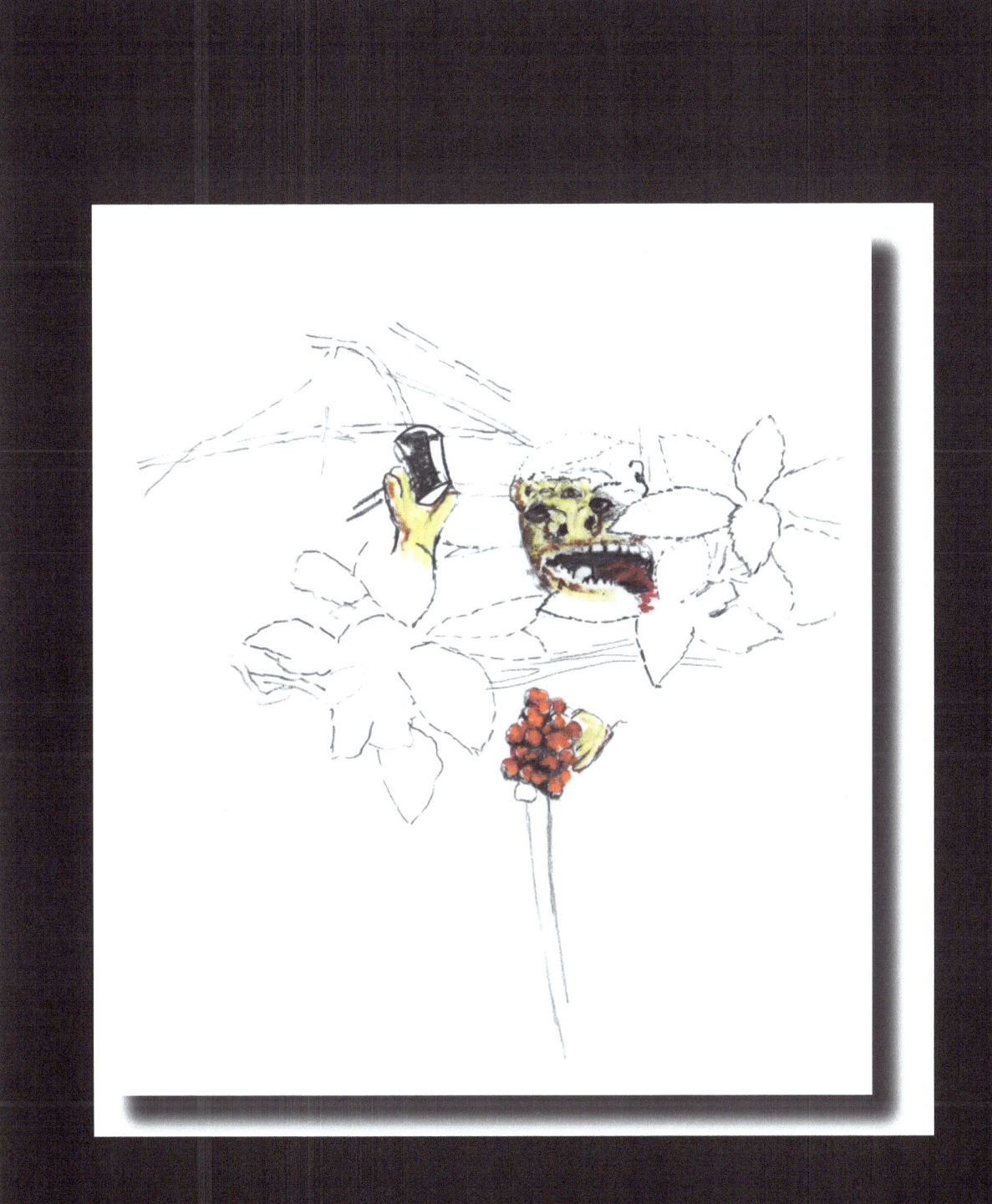

URU-HAI ORCS

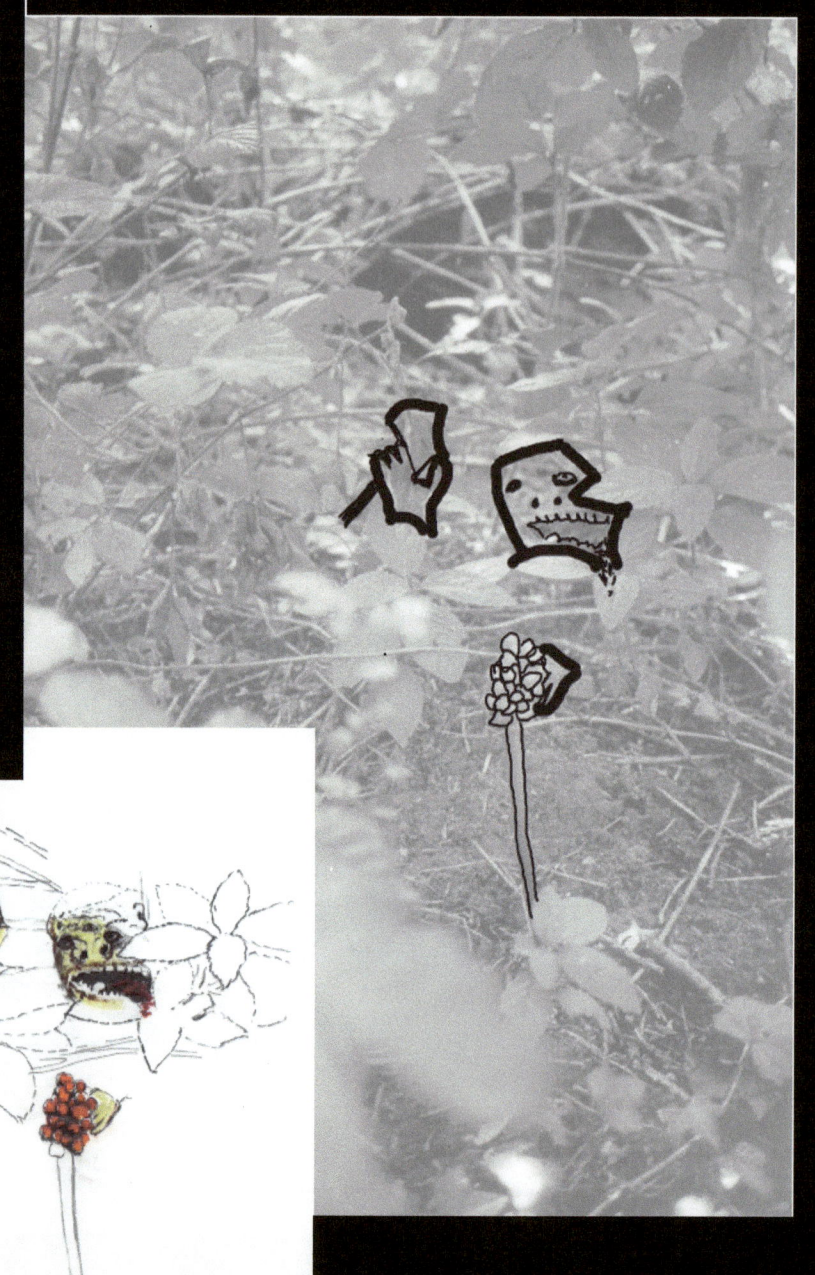

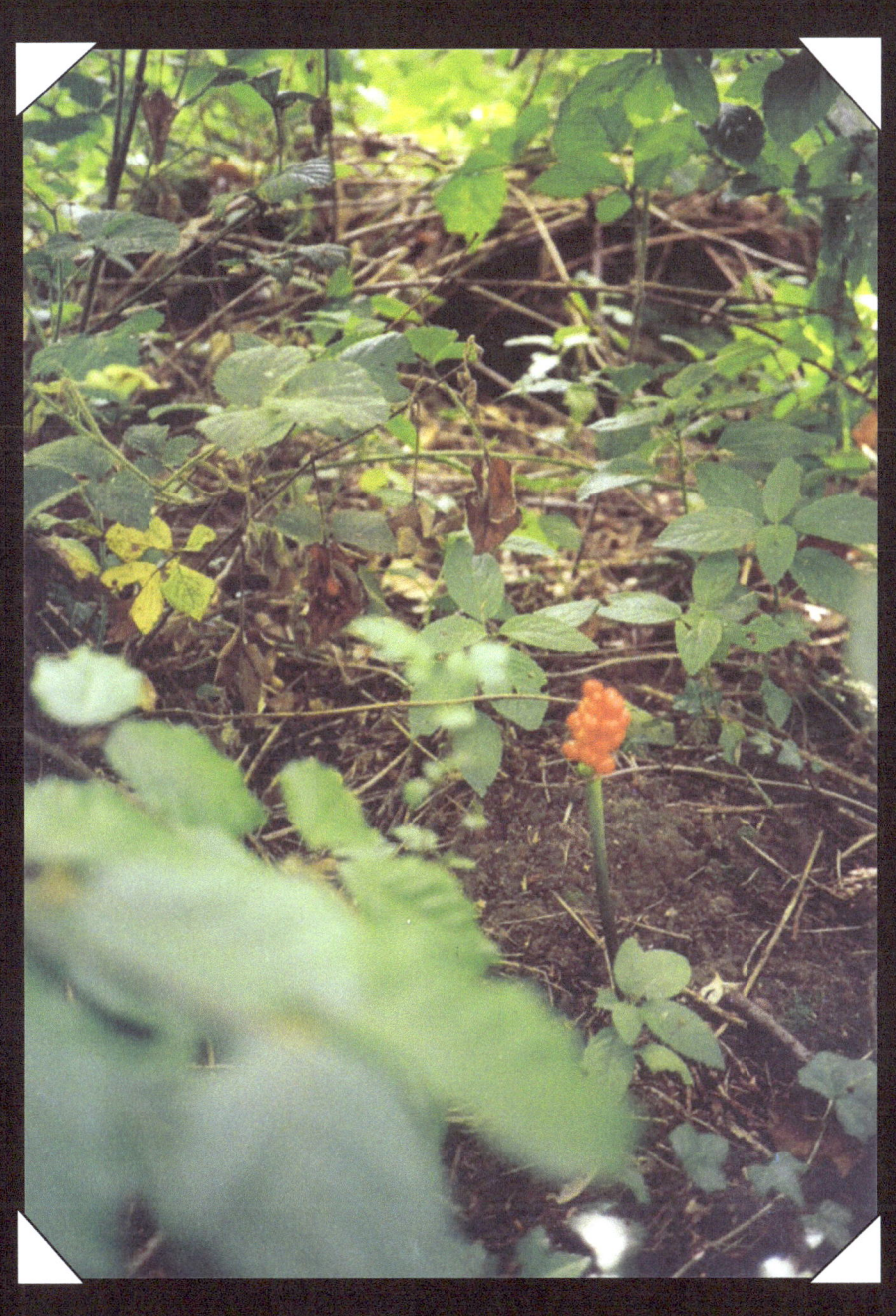

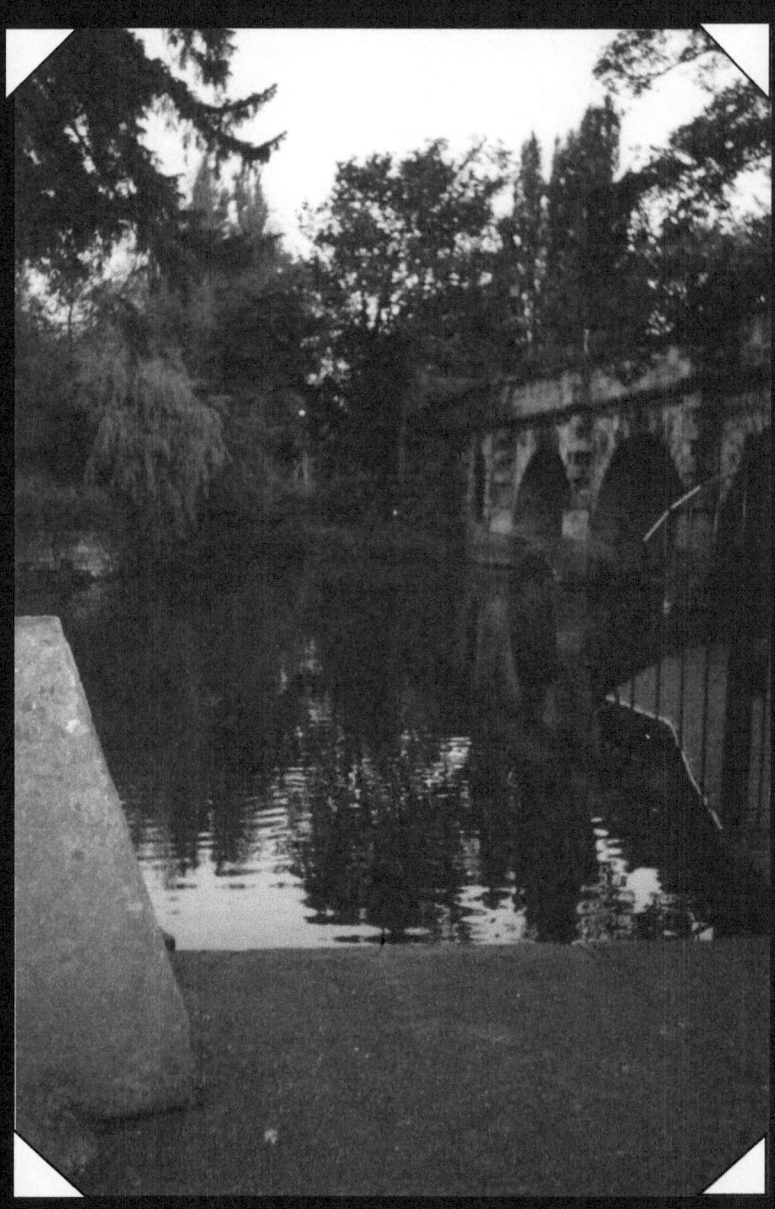

What do you see?

BOTH GOOD AND BAD

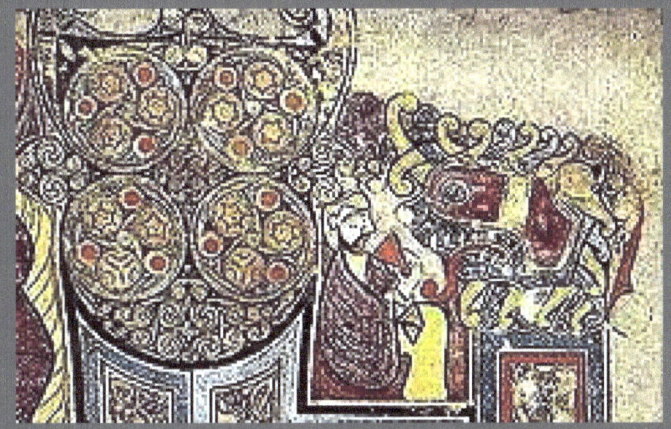

Book of Kells illustration Circa 800 (public domain)

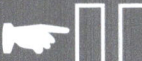 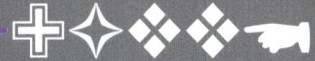

GOLLUM

The path that Lewis and Tolkien undoubtedly walked together from their homes in Headington to their colleges In Oxford passes through deserted fields and shady areas.

There is a particular stream darkened by overhanging trees and bushes where you might encounter a strange being, Listen carefully for splashing noises that sound like birds or overzealous fish. If you look carefully you may be surprised to see a white hand reaching out from beneath the water. Focus on a floating branch close by and realize that at the end of it is a a little white foot! You will probably hear the words, "My precious, my precious....."

--- Depraved, Corrupted ---

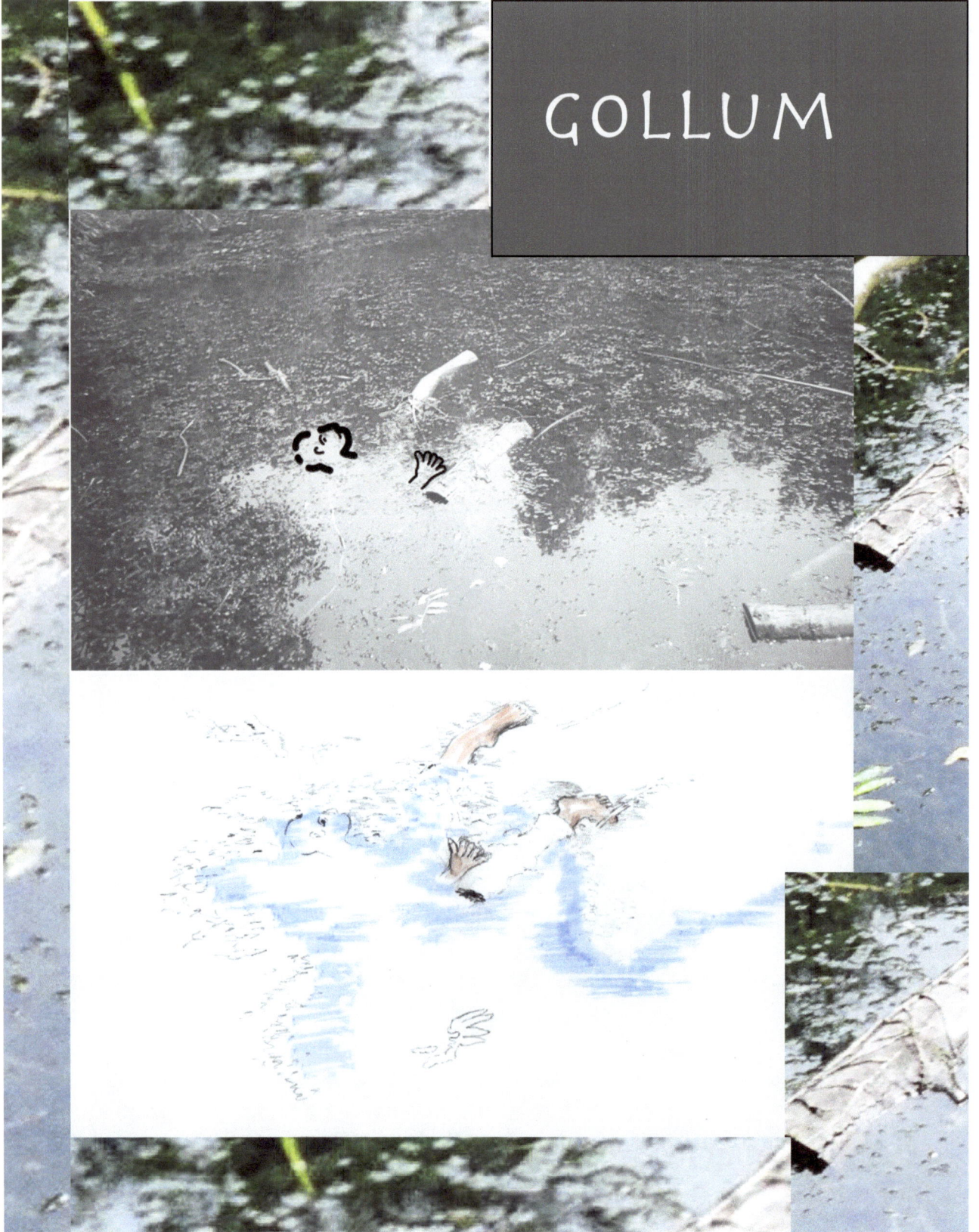

GOLLUM

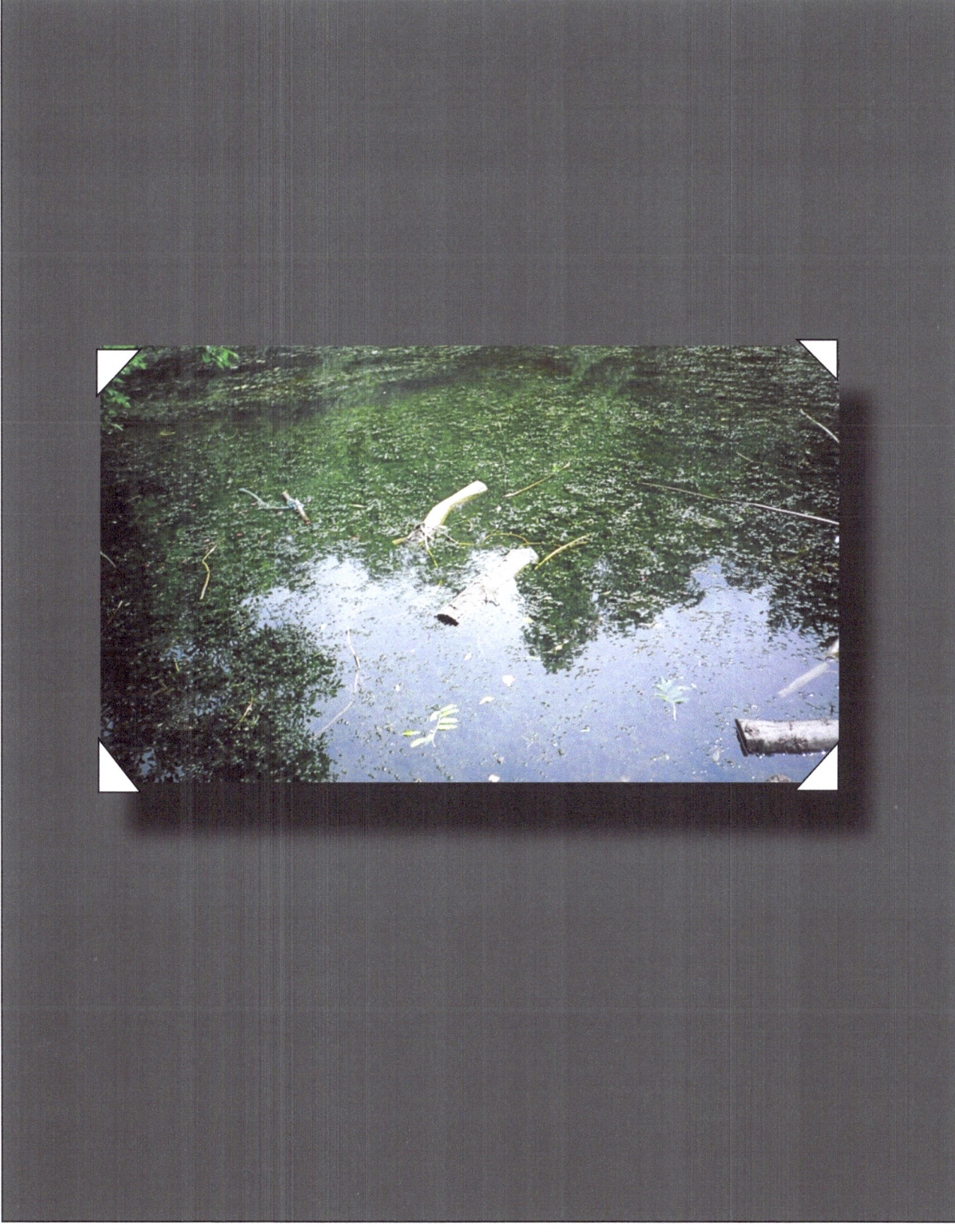

HUMANS

Why not decide to
RETURN TO YOUR IMAGINATION
and open a door to a whole new world?

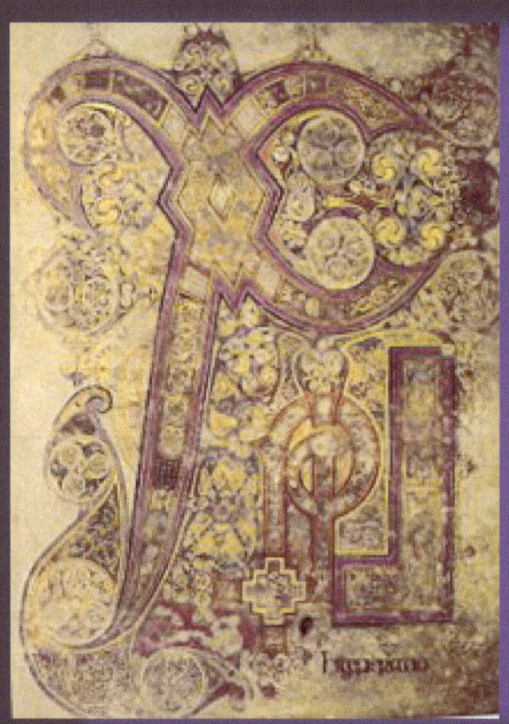

Book of Kells folio 034 Circa 800 (public domain)

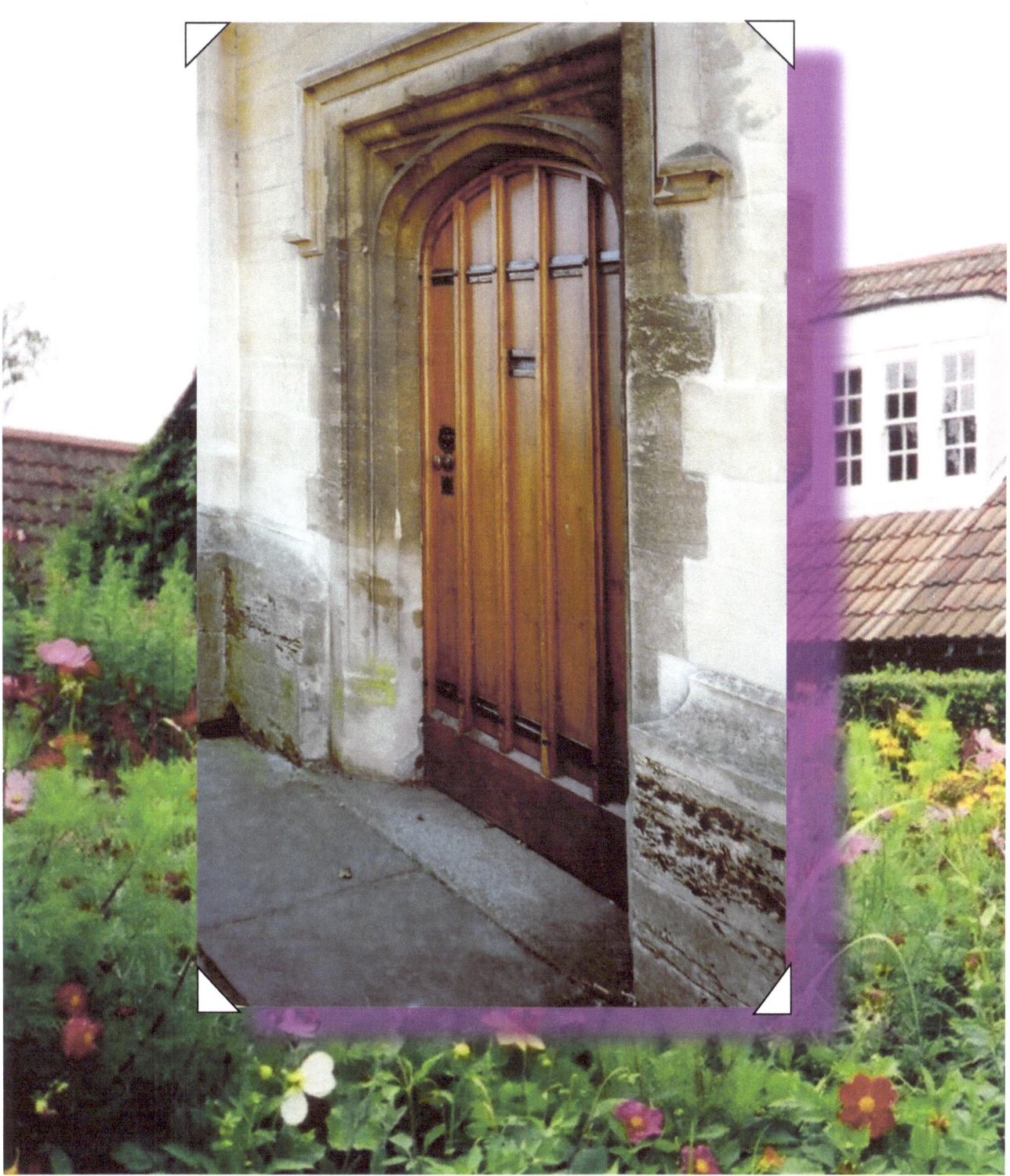

Lewis' "front yard" on Shotover Hill offers the magic to inspire imagination. Legend has it that, in earlier times, the famous Romantic English poet, Shelley, gained inspiration roaming these very woods. Countless other artists and poets have long recorded their sense of the numinous and dynamic qualities of distinctively beautiful landscapes such as Shotover Hill.

With a return to imagination, an adult can regain part of what had been lost with the passing of childhood. Lewis and Tolkien used their imagination to write stories unique in their time. Tolkien's stories (with characters noted in this book) may seem childlike but these epic adventures are now ranked among the most popular adult novels of the past century.

In the same way as Tolkien, and as Lewis, we ourselves can use the vehicle of our imagination to free ourselves from the confined, narrow scenes of daily life, moving instead towards the rich expansive vision of an exhilarating, newly alive world. Although the creative process, itself, is a myst ery, we can enrich our own lives by following the lead of these literary giants. Putting aside preconceived ideas and ordinary logic, we can begin to ....

ignite the passions
of your imagination!

You are invited

no, urged

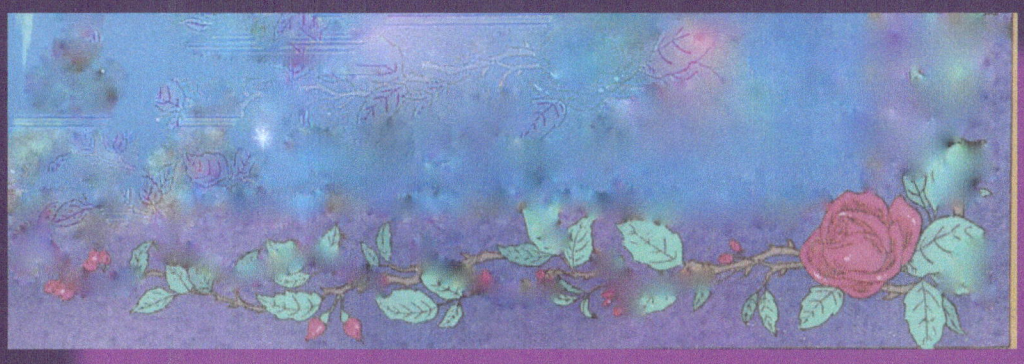

to fully use your personal imagination

and celebrate the creativity of

the world of

"Faerie."

Tolkin Pictures

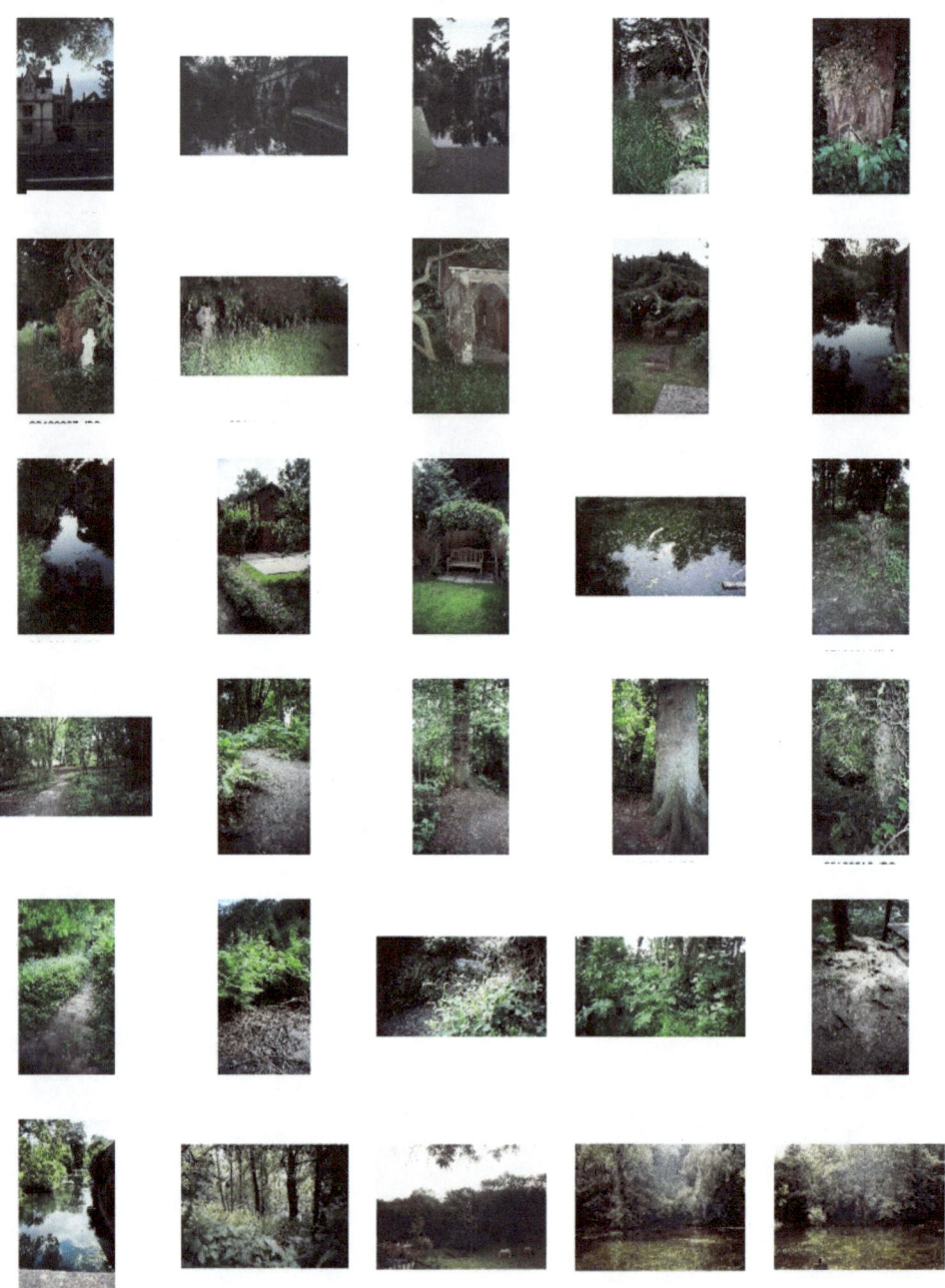

Photographs taken in Oxford, England by Shari G. Grant

www.ingramcontent.com/pod-product-compliance
Lightning Source LLC
Chambersburg PA
CBHW050734180526
45159CB00003B/1226